Saratoga's Great Ladies
Broadway and Franklin Square
with State Street and Greenfield Avenue

First edition

By

Hollis A. Palmer Ph.D.

Deep Roots Publications
Saratoga Springs, New York 12866

Saratoga's Great Ladies
Broadway and Franklin Square

Published by
Deep Roots Publications
P.O. Box 114
Saratoga Springs, New York

Library of Congress Number 2006906629
Printed in the United States of America

ISBN 09671713-4-2

This book is dedicated to my first great lady
my mother

Doris Wooddell Palmer

Special thanks to

Heather Barrett

For refining my words that it looks like
I knew these people,

And to

Jim Russo

Who had to work harder this time because we both
wanted this book to look so good.

Table of Contents

Letter to the reader

It is anticipated that this will be the first in a series of books about the families that turned the houses into homes; those homes into a community and that community into the Saratoga we know today. It is anticipated that the work will take six to seven volumes and the same number of years. While considering taking on a project of this magnitude of this series it became apparent that I needed to know why I wanted undertake the task and what would be included in the series. Wanting to share my appreciation of Saratoga clarified my motivation was clear; I wanted to get as many people interested in the history of the city as possible. It is my observation that people enjoy learning about people more than facts; therefore, the books would focus on the people and the role they played in the events that molded the city. I also understood that no matter what was finally published there would be people who would criticize the work. Weighing the task against the returns, which include the inevitable detractors, I decided that this was one way to express my respect for the city, and I would let others find there own way.

My admiration of the city runs deep. Like my father, his father, his father and even his father before him, as a young child I lived in South Glens Falls. Unlike those four generations, at the time I entered junior high school my family moved from the area. Several times each year we would travel through Saratoga on our way back to our former home to visit family and friends. Each trip I would beg my father, who was always the driver, to take what we called the back route going by the grand Victorian Houses on Clement Street and North Broadway. Now as I reflect on the conversations that took place as we drove by the homes and with my grandfather later, I realize that it was not the architecture that drew me to want to take this side trip but rather it was the stories of the people who lived in the "cottages." Even then my interest was in the families who had amassed fortunes large enough to allow them to live in such grandeur. This series is an attempt to excite others about Saratoga's rich history by telling stories of the families that built and lived in these fine houses.

People who appreciate history and historians are not necessarily the same. Historians do more than just know about events they add perspective and interpretation for others. Through this series and my other books I feel that I am an historian.

My observation is that people who appreciate history fall into two distinct camps. There are those who hoard history, collecting and keeping things to themselves. One of those "historians" stole my great-great-great-great-great-grandfather's will from the county records. The other group want to share history; seeing their roles as a vehicle to interest others in our collective past. I hope I am considered in the second group; only time will determine the appropriate classification.

There are people who put things together and people who pick things apart. When you hear someone, stress a story that they heard differently from what is included in this book note it. Write it on a sheet of paper and put in the book. Better yet take your note to the Saratoga History Room at the library. Our history, even our oral history, has to be recorded before it is lost.

The focus of this book is on the families that built the homes and therefore the city. To understand the families it is sometimes important to digress and explain why the investments and decisions they made were important.

Remember this book was written to be a peek into the lives of those who came before us not a full blown biography of any individual.

The ideas and opinions expressed in this text are those of the author. They are based on extensive reading, more extensive observations, and a desire to add a perspective to a city I have always liked and come to love.

I hope you enjoy the book, as I enjoyed discovering the stories myself.

Hollis Palmer

All readers who use this book as a guide for a walking tour are reminded that many of these buildings are still private residences and the owners have a right to privacy; please be respectful.

An idea develops into a series

Traveling on Union Avenue, Circular Street or North Broadway one can not help but find his or her eyes fixated on the gracious Victorian houses that adorn each street. For me it was after leaving the main thoroughfares and exploring the streets such as Marion Place, Fifth Avenue, Franklin Square, Caroline, Phila, and Spring Streets that I started to wonder about the families that initially built and owned these intriguing homes. With the first book in the series: **Saratoga's Great Ladies** finished, I can assure you that it was as enjoyable to journey back in time and learn about these families as it is to walk among the houses they left behind.

The original idea was to have one book, which would cover about 200 houses. In walking the streets trying to select the houses to include, it became apparent that there were over 400 houses that should be discussed. The issue became whether to do one book that would be awkward to carry or to publish multiple books. As the research progressed, it was recognized that there were not 400 houses but rather 600 to 800 houses that deserved to have their history recorded. The decision was to do multiple books, each covering specific streets. To make the first book a loop, **Saratoga's Great Ladies: Broadway and Franklin Square** also includes part of State Street and Greenfield Avenue. The second book in the series **Saratoga's Great Ladies: Merchants and Mansions** will include the first twelve houses on Circular Street, Phila Street out even when it becomes Fifth Avenue and Union Avenue. Later books will include other streets such as Spring, Caroline, Regent along with Marion, Madison, Lake, Nelson, Clinton and Clement. One of the last books will be devoted to the buildings that were not houses; the casino, race track, and most of the buildings downtown.

Terms that have changed meanings

In this series there are families living in houses well beyond the means of people with similar titles today. That is a result of new titles being added at the top and what was a more professional title in the 1800s has been diminished. An example is the Victorian title "head bookkeeper," which today would be the Chief Financial Officer.

It seems Americans need to keep creating new titles so that the old titles can be shared by more people.

A second phenomenon appears more in future volumes but is in the replacement of occupations. Some changes were logical such as carriage makers becoming body shops and harness shops becoming auto parts stores. Others are basically new, such as plumber and electrician.

Bookkeeper – The bookkeeper had a greater range of responsibilities than the same title has today. In a time before calculators, computers and when business was usually done in cash, the bookkeeper had responsibility for the owner's records and finances. This was often the position that a close family member who was going to take over the business, held before ascending to proprietor.

Brevet – At the end of the Civil War many officers were promoted one or more ranks either at the time of their discharge or even following their actual service. Such promotions were usually done in honor for the person's service. The advantage was that years later, if they applied for a pension, they were able to claim based on the higher rank.

Military rank – Following the Civil War, many ex-servicemen used their title for the rest of their lives. People in a community were referred to as the Captain or Colonel rather than their first name. In smaller communities the titles were not even followed by the person's last name – there was after all only one General. The assignment of rank as a nickname was a sign of respect.

President (of a bank or company) – The title president of small companies and even banks, referred to the person who was president of the board of directors. The same person was universally a stock holder and often held the largest block of stock. The president rarely had day-to-day supervisory responsibilities; those were left to the tellers in banks and superintendents in manufacturing concerns. Those with other titles such as vice president and treasurer were usually other large stockholders.

Proprietor – of a hotel – was the person who operated the hotel on a day-by-day basis. Since many of the hotels were leased by professional managers, the proprietor may or may not have been the owner. Since the hotels were not chains and operated on the American Plan, the proprietor actively mixed with the clientele.

Superintendent – Before the title manager, which even today is sometimes replaced with vice president, manufacturing concerns, and bottling plants were operated by the superintendent. It seems Americans need to keep creating new titles so that the old titles can be shared by more people.

Teller – Banks dealt in cash. When the grand hotels made deposits, lots of cash! As noted before, the president of the bank did not work in the bank on a daily basis. The title teller would be comparable to a branch manager today or even to president of a small bank.

Franklin
Square

Although there may be individual houses in Saratoga that are older than those in Franklin Square, no neighborhood has as many historically significant homes in one enclave. The five houses that surround this plaza were the residences of representatives from most of the "first families" of the village. Standing almost anywhere in the square one can see the homes of judges, congressmen, entrepreneurs, military leaders and people in the professions. One hundred and fifty years ago, these were the homes of some of the wealthiest of Saratoga's year-round residents.

Franklin Square shows that preservation can work even amid rapid growth. If there was a way to remove the cars from the Square one would soon have the sense that time had frozen. Here, in the mist of some of Saratoga's most brisk building growth, there are older homes nestled together as if, through unity, they have been able to stay off development or worse yet, the wrecking ball.

Today, while in the square, one might regret: being in the shadow of the new condominiums; the noise that seems to never end; or even the seemingly confusing traffic brought on by proximity to Broadway and openness of the square. Each of these distractions are now less than their counterparts were a hundred years ago. The United States Hotel was six stories tall, casting a silhouette at least as long as the buildings that replaced it. The train station was in the area immediately to the east of the square. The sounds of the trains, the wagons and carriages that were constantly picking up and dropping off travelers combined with the constant yelling by the hack drivers, would make today's volume seem serene. Cab drivers may appear not to follow the rules of the road; however, when one considers what it was like to deal with the same personality in the old hack drivers combined with the nervousness of a team of horses, it is obvious the confusion has decreased.

Two of the houses (3 & 4) were owned by the Marvin brothers. Later the houses were lived in by the cousins and their spouses. Members of these families were responsible for hotels, banks, insurance companies and some of the regional railroads. Unlike Union Avenue and North Broadway where some houses were seasonal "cottages," the residences of this neighborhood lived, worked, and worshiped in the village; they were Saratogians.

Researching those who built and lived in the houses on this square, one sees once again that even when the residents were year-round they were rarely native to Saratoga. Dr. McEwen (1) was born in Connecticut, coming to Saratoga for his own health (it worked-he lived another 30 years). George Harvey (2) was not born in the village. The Marvin brothers (3 & 4) were born in Ballston Spa and moved to the village as adults. Joel Clements (5), who married into the Putnam family, moved to Saratoga from Vermont. Examining the history of the families in just these houses, it becomes obvious that Saratoga has a unique ability to redefine itself, grow, and prosper through a variety of different economic conditions.

FRANKLIN SQ.

1

Dr. McEwen

This house was purchased by Dr. Robert McEwen in the late 1860s. With its attached side rooms the house was typical of those owned by a doctor or lawyer who wanted an office attached to his home. The professional person lived in the center section and one side room of the house, and his public office was in the other side room with a separate entrance.

Intelligent, driven, and dedicated, Dr. McEwen was not someone meant to live a traditional life. Born in 1833 in rural Bainbridge, New York, McEwen left in search of the best classical education. For his time and profession he was well educated graduating from Williams College before attending lectures at Yale University. Set on the field of medicine, he went to New York College of Physicians and Surgeons where he graduated in the mid 1850s (most doctors at the time were still learning the profession by working with other physicians).

Dr. McEwen began his practice as the house physician for Bellevue Hospital. He held that position for a year and a half before he accepted a commission on behalf of the British Government to serve as a surgeon in South America.

By 1860 McEwen was back in the United States practicing medicine in Stamford, Connecticut. With the onset of hostilities McEwen joined the 17th Connecticut Volunteers. He was only able to serve for two years before his personal health gave out. Forced to resign his commission, he did not give up his commitment to military service and even when he lived in Saratoga he had a commission in the reserves. It took several years, but eventually he was successful in his efforts to have the state establish an armory in the city (the building that is now the State Military History Museum). The State paid $40,000 for the construction and the city provided the land, which was valued at $10,000.

In 1865 he married Caroline Armstrong by whom he had one daughter, Jennie. Suffering from the effects of his own service, Dr. McEwen decided that it would be in the best interest of his entire family's health to move to Saratoga. They arrived in 1866. The move did not have the positive effect so eagerly anticipated and he was widowed the next year; he also lost his daughter.

Having no connections to other places Dr. McEwen remained in Saratoga where, on June 10, 1867, he married Sarah Watrous of Troy. They had two children: Robert Jr. who lived less than a year, and Ellen born 1875. Dr. McEwen died when he was sixty on Dec. 26, 1893. The McEwen's daughter, Ellen, died a little over three years later. She was approximately twenty-one.

Sarah was stronger. With her entire family gone, Sarah sold this house and moved across the street where she opened a boarding house. Her new residence at 2 Franklin did not have the dimensions that it has now.

Sarah would live an additional twenty years, dying October of 1917.

FRANKLIN SQ.

2

G. Harvey

This building had neither the dimensions nor opulence of the current structure when, in the 1870s, it was the home of George Harvey. A lumber dealer and a generation older than George F. Harvey, the relationship between the two George Harveys has not been established; although, the fact that there were two may explain why the one who was in the pharmaceutical business used his middle initial.

In the 1870 census the George Harvey who resided here listed the value of his property at $50,000 and his total worth at $80,000; a sizable net value at the time. The Harvey family lived in this house with a cook, maid and teamster. He and his wife had one son, Henry, living home. Henry was a clerk at the family's lumber yard on Division Street.

The 1850s and 1860s was a time to be a lumber merchant in Saratoga. The hotels were expanding and, in the case of the Congress and United States, needed to be rebuilt following fires. Additionally, the "cottages" on Broadway were being built and other businesses growing.

Harvey was a deeply religious man. He was one of the first non-ministers who served as president of the Saratoga County Bible Society and for ten years, 1858-68, he was treasurer of the Sons of Temperance Society.

The record on what happened to this George Harvey is hard to trace since it does not appear that he was in the county when he died.

3 & 4

James Madison
Marvin
Thomas Marvin

The stories of the two Marvin brothers' families, who lived at numbers 3 and 4 Franklin Square, are told together because they are an integrated story. In terms of investments, political involvement and their children's continued commitment to the city, their lives were similar; yet, as is always the case in other ways their lives were different. Because they were a force behind so many initiatives in Saratoga, and because their influence was so great, their tale is told jointly.

When the Marvin family moved to Upstate New York from Connecticut they originally settled near Ballston Spa. Two of their sons, Thomas and James, would move to Saratoga, where their impact would last long after they had expired. The reason for the move was in part because of their mother's brother Elias Benedict. Elias was the man who originally owned the land that constitutes the block along Broadway between Washington and Division Street. He built the first United States Hotel. Later, the Marvin brothers would become partners in the hotel.

Today it is common for people to name their children after friends, family or even characters from books, television, movies or celebrities. Following the Revolutionary War a family showed their commitment to the new country by naming their children after the nation's founding fathers; thus, we have James Madison Marvin (3) and Thomas Jefferson Marvin (4). Thomas was born in 1803, the year of the Louisiana Purchase and while Thomas Jefferson was President. James was six years younger; born in 1809, the year Madison became President. These brothers would show their commitment to the country's ideals by building houses with tall

pillars designed similar to the White House and they would name their hotel The United States.

Thomas graduated from Union College in 1824 coming to Saratoga to study law in the office of William Warren. He was accepted before the bar in 1828. As was expected of men in the professions and even successful businessmen, Thomas was active in politics and social causes. Within Saratoga his community service started when he was justice of the peace and went on to service as a village trustee and even president of the village (equivalent to mayor). He was elected to the State Assembly, served as a supervisor on the county legislature and elected county judge. He also served in the very lucrative position of postmaster. Although accounts hold that he served each political office with distinction, it was his business interests that had a more dramatic influence on Saratoga.

During his short lifetime (he died in 1852 at the age of 49), Thomas received the first state charter for a mutual fire insurance company (later to become Saratoga Mutual), created the first bank in the village, was instrumental in the railroads and was part owner of the village's best lodgings: the United States Hotel.

James, the younger brother, came to Saratoga in 1838 at the age of 19 to work for his uncle who had controlling interest in the United States Hotel. He moved for one year to Albany where he remained in the hotel business. Returning to Saratoga in 1840, he became the proprietor of the United States Hotel.

Like his brother, James Marvin was active in local affairs. Starting as a volunteer fireman, he would later serve on the county legislature including one term as chairman. James would go on to be a State Assemblyman before being elected to the United States

Congress during the Civil War. He served six years in Congress from 1862 until 1868. When the village decided to build the reservoir and install a water system village, James was the commissioner of the water works.

In addition to being the proprietor of the hotel and director of the bank he opened with his brother, James was a director of two local railroads and after the merger he was a director of the New York Central.

The United States Hotel

The most visible business of the Marvin family was the United States Hotel. The hotel had stood directly across the street from the old train station and was literally one of the first buildings visitors saw when they disembarked from the train. Built in the 1820s, the hotel would stand as a gateway to the great hotels until it burned in 1865.

The fire was in mid-June, just as the season was beginning to peak. Late in the afternoon, the fire started in the attic area. Since fire burns up, it spread very slowly at first allowing time for most of the furniture and guest personal property to be saved. Once the fire dropped to the lower floors it spread rapidly. With winds from the southwest, the flames jumped Division Street and the Marvin House (a smaller hotel not owned by the family) also burned to the ground. The first building that was saved was the Davison House (Wine Bar). Two people died as a result of the fire; one, a policeman who was killed when the chimney fell on him.

The destruction of the hotel was a major setback for the city and the Marvin family. The hotel loss was estimated at $300,000 but since it was assumed that any fire would be put out before it could destroy the entire structure the insurance was only for $110,000.

The problem with the settlement and rebuilding was the result of the hotel never being owned by one person. Although from 1840 on James was almost always one of the proprietors, over the years he had a series of partners. At the time of the fire, James and his brother's estate owned over half of the hotel; their Uncle Lewis Benedict's estate owned most of the rest. Because ownership was tied up in the two estates, over thirty people claimed a share of the insurance and loss.

James, who was occupied as a Congressman at the time, started to have the debris cleaned up immediately. Rumors started that Major Leland, the new proprietor of the Union Hotel, was trying to limit competition by getting to some of the more distant Marvin family members encouraging them to slow down the rebuilding process. The truth of the rumors can not be determined a hundred and fifty years later but we do know that the hotel was not rebuilt for nine years.

1865 was the first season following the end of the Civil War, and was projected to be a celebration with all the hotels prospering. Guests to the village that summer were greeted by not only the rubble of the once grand hotel but the smell of the recent fire.

When the United States was finally rebuilt it surpassed any of its contemporaries. On its grand piazza Commodore Vanderbilt would "hold court." Each day on the hotel's porches and in its gardens deals would be made; fortunes would be won and lost; young couples would be introduced; fortune hunters would try to meet heiresses; and widows would sit as dowagers surveying the behavior of those they found acceptable and those who were beneath their scope.

The Marvin Families

Thomas (4 FS), the older brother, died in December of 1852 in Havana, Cuba, probably as the result of tuberculosis. He had been sick for several years and that year had gone south to avoid a northeastern winter. Following Thomas' death his brother, James, would assume responsibility for both families.

Out of respect for their father, both Thomas and James named their only sons William. Both boys died before they reached their tenth birthday. James and Thomas each had several daughters. The children from both families would impact the city.

3 Franklin Square

James Marvin had four daughters: Mary (b. 1839), Frances (b. 1841), Caroline (b. 1843), and Rhoby (b. 1858), named for her mother. Mary married Charles Meehan and had two sons. Charles died before 1875, and Mary remarried Dr. Charles Payn, a dentist in the village. In the 1850s and early 1860s Dr, Payn had been a partner in the Union Hotel. After the Payns married they moved to Paris, France for three years. Dr. Payn, who was almost the same age as Mary's father, would die in 1881. She lived until 1918 and never remarried.

Frances married Murray Colgate Shoemaker, a lawyer from Cincinnati, Ohio. Frances would live most of her adult life in Ohio, where she remained close to members of the Clement Family from 5 Franklin Square. Murray Shoemakers father, Robert, was one of the early builders of the railroads in Ohio. The Shoemaker's were reasonably wealthy. Even after the Murray death in 1885, Frances continued to have at least three servants. Their son, also named Murray, was a lawyer like his father. Her daughter, Henrietta, was the first wife of Nash Rockwood (31 Union) whose divorce was so infamous that it made the New York Times.

Caroline married William B. Gage (779 Br) who, after the United States Hotel was rebuilt, would be a proprietor with John Perry, the husband of his wife's cousin, and Henry Thompson. James was no longer listed as one of the proprietors.

The last daughter, Rhoby, has proven difficult to trace.

James Madison Marvin died in 1901 at the age of 92. At the time of his death two of his daughters, Frances and Mary, were residing with him. The sisters were both widowed. Following their father's death Frances would return to Cincinnati and Mary would remain in the family home. The third sister, Caroline Gage, was living at 779 Broadway.

4 Franklin Square

In addition to their son who died before he was three, Thomas Marvin and his wife, Harriett, had three daughters. The girls were Mary (b.1840), Virginia (b. 1843), and Grace (b. 1846). Grace died in 1862 at age 16; she never had the chance to marry.

The effect on girls age 12, 9 and 6 in watching a vibrant father lose his strength can only be estimated. Their ultimate relationship may cause one to wonder about the bond the loss created. Thomas Marvin left four women behind; none would ever live any place except in the house on Franklin Square.

The two daughters who lived to be adults were Mary and Virginia. They would have an interesting relationship; they would both marry dynamic men. Neither of the sisters would have children and they would live in the same house together until 1895 when the first one died. This extended relationship may explain why the house constructed was so long.

In 1864, Virginia, the second born, was the first to marry. She married Dr. John L. Perry, son of Dr. John Perry (377 Br). Perry, who was a native Saratogian, had served as the assistant surgeon in the 115th NY Volunteers. While in the service he contracted typhus and was forced to resign his commission. His active service over, Perry started a private practice in the village and was in charge of the medical department of the 2nd Veteran Calvary; a unit assigned to Saratoga. Shortly after his wedding Perry's health issues returned and he gave up his medical practice. He and his wife traveled around Europe seeking a cure for his reoccurring fever. In 1866 his health was much better and the Perrys returned to Saratoga. John Perry purchased part ownership in a local pharmacy which he maintained until 1873.

In 1874, he joined in a partnership with several other prominent Saratogians including William Gage, the husband of his wife's cousin, in reopening the United States Hotel. Perry's ability to speak fluent French, German and Spanish, combined with his managerial skills and world travels made him an asset to the rebuilt hotel. Perry and Gage would remain as the proprietors of the hotel until Perry's death in 1915.

In 1876, sixty-five year old William Sackett married thirty- six year old Mary Louise Marvin. Sackett, who was only ten years younger than Mary's father, had much in common with both the Marvin men. William was a lawyer (the same as Thomas); he had served in Congress from 1849 -1853 (the same as James). Sackett had been married twice before and had seven children by his first two wives. When William Sackett married Mary Marvin, he had lost three children of his own; the same number as James and Thomas combined.

Sackett had moved to Saratoga in 1853, immediately after he finished his term as a Congressman. Sackett had invested well and did not practice law after his move to the village. Like the second generation of the Marvins, Sackett's children by his previous marriages were scattered around the state and country.

William's oldest son, Col. William Sackett (b. 1838), was an attorney practicing law in Albany at the start of the Civil War. He enlisted and was promoted to Colonel of the 9th New York Calvary. His troops, while serving as pickets, fired the first shots at the Battle of Gettysburg. William was killed in the Battle of Trevilian Station June 9, 1864. He was given a posthumous promotion to General.

Sackett's other children were; Edward Sackett, a lawyer in Seneca Falls; Mrs. Charles Stone, the wife of a lawyer in Syracuse; Mrs. Charles Duell, whose husband was commissioner of patents; Mrs. Lighthall, who lived in Geneva. Sackett's remaining son, Frederick, died in California in 1887.

With his marriage to Mary Louise Marvin, Sackett began a three year tour of Europe. He recorded the trip in a series of letters which were published in journals.

William Sackett and his sister-in-law, Virginia Perry, both died in 1895. John Perry would continue as a proprietor of the hotel but would move out of the house in Franklin Square. For the next thirty years Mary Marvin Sackett would be the only family member to live in the house. She died in 1926.

The Lincoln Avenue gates to Greenridge Cemetery are dedicated to the Sacketts.

5

Clement/
Olmstead

In 1868 the *Saratogian* started the obituary, "It is our painful duty to announce the death of Joel Clement one our oldest and most highly respected citizens." There were reasons the newspaper had so much praise for Clement. In 1818 he had been on one of the first school committees (later replaced by school boards); in 1822 he was the town clerk; in 1830 when Bethesda Church was organized he was a vestryman; and from 1838-43 treasurer of the village; all these were nonpaying responsibilities.

Clement reached the age of 83 and had lived in Saratoga for almost 60 years. When Clement arrived in 1809 Putnam's Tavern had been built but Gideon Putnam had not yet started Congress Hall. Joel was a business person investing in several enterprises, especially the first railroads. Joel would marry one of Putnam's daughters, Aurelia; together they would have five children. Both their sons, John and William, would move to Cincinnati. William, a civil engineer, would become the president of a railroad; in 1870 he would list his worth at $200,000. Their daughter Mary would die unmarried. No record could be found on their daughter Frances.

When Joel Clement died he left the house to Caroline Olmstead, his only child still living in Saratoga. In 1849 Caroline, who was in her early twenties, married a local attorney, Aaron Olmstead, who was 38. Caroline is one of the founders of the Home of the Good Shepard but, in the chauvinistic style of the day, her husband was the one selected to serve on the board of directors.

The Olmsteads had two daughters both of whom moved out of the community and the family legacy was lost.

The house was once two stories tall but following a fire was refurbished on one level.

Broadway

Broadway is one of the best examples of both the nature of the growth of Saratoga Springs and how the city renews and reinvents itself. Until the 1940s the site across from Congress Park was where The Grand Union Hotel stood. The Grand Union had replaced the Union hotel. When the Grand Union was torn down, a typical benign plaza was built that rented space to a grocery store named the Grand Union and other small businesses. In the 1990s the plaza was razed and where the Grand Union Hotel once stood with stores on the ground floor and rooms above, there is now an impressive brick building with stores on the first floor and a business above. Further up the street at the corner of Division Street, the United States Hotel has been replaced by stores and condominiums. The corner of Spring and Broadway, the site of the former Congress Hotel, is now an art center and park. Renewal is not new; City Hall, which was built in 1871, stands on the site of the Pavilion, one of the earliest hotels that had burned. The Post Office and Adirondack Trust buildings appear venerable today but replaced homes that had become outdated. Even on North Broadway almost all the homes that have been built since 1950 replaced houses that had either burned or were demolished.

In many ways the houses on Broadway reflect Saratoga as it expanded and need changed in purposes of the houses. The oldest houses are 377 and 425. These homes were in the heart of the old village near the three biggest hotels: Grand Union, Congress, and United States. As one goes out Broadway in either direction, the houses are newer (a relative term since we are still talking 130 years ago). In the area considered downtown there are several old row houses (425, 465, 489, 491, and 493). These houses were built for people in the professions or who had commercial interest in the city. These professionals had residences on the upper floors with their offices on ground level. In contrast the first block on North Broadway, which are newer homes, are the houses built for professional people whose offices were not in their homes.

At opposite ends of Broadway stands The Washington Inn to the south and Redstone Villa to the north. Each of these houses was built as a cottage for families who spent the "season" in Saratoga. Many of the homes on the upper blocks of North Broadway were the "cottages" of industrialists, bankers and brokers who used them only in the summer season. While the houses closer to downtown were built as year-round residences.

At the time of this writing, over the length of Broadway there are still 58 buildings that were built prior to 1920 and started out as private residences. Amazingly and probably unique to Saratoga, the majority of these great ladies are still private residences; however, because of their commercial locations several former townhouses now accommodate businesses and professional offices instead of families.

Many of the buildings had to adapt to survive. Away from the center of Broadway one of the former houses is now an inn; one a bed and breakfast; and one is the private guest house for a local business. Other former homes have become offices, restaurants and one was even a convent for a period. At one point the sheer size of some of these "Victorian Cottages" and the economy required that they become apartment houses or they would have been lost to history.

A touch of history

Broadway owes its unusual breath to the wisdom of Gideon Putnam who had a vision for Saratoga as a resort. In a time of horse drawn carriages, Putnam laid out a main street 120 feet wide. A visit to almost any other post colonial community would show how different these dimensions are as compared to other streets constructed at the same time.

Despite common references to North and South Broadway, the houses are continuously numbered and there is officially only one Broadway. In 1874, approximately the middle of the American Victorian Era, a *New York Times* article defined South Broadway as the area south of Circular Street; Broadway was considered to be the area from Circular Street to the railroad tracks (Van Dam); North Broadway was the remainder of the street north of the railroad tracks. A hundred-thirty years later those same reference points persist.

The 1874 *Times* article that defined Broadway discussed the rapid growth in Saratoga. During preceding twelve months; 264 "cottages" had been built.

BROADWAY

417

G. Davison

The townhouse of Gideon Davison is one of the oldest houses in this book (c 1825). When this house was constructed it was common for the residences of small businessmen to serve as both a home and the business site. The Davison family lived in the upper two floors and the printing business was in the raised basement. Built with detailed brick work, the bay windows above the door and on the side were a later renovation.

Prior to arriving in Saratoga, Davison, who was trained as a printer, was living in Vermont where he and a partner published the *Rutland Herald,* a newspaper still in circulation. Davison saw Saratoga as a place that was growing and where he could start a new newspaper. Since most of his revenue would be from advertisements, Davison needed to be sure that businesses would support his investment. Davison first visited Saratoga to seek out the support of some of the more influential men of the community; a common practice at the time. Assured of their backing, at the age of twenty-seven, Davison moved to Saratoga. In April of 1818, the first edition of the *Saratoga Sentinel,* a weekly newspaper, was printed.

When Davison began publishing the *Sentinel,* newspapers were brazenly political. During the period that Davison owned the *Sentinel,* there was a deep philosophical division between the Federalist Party (John Adams) and the Democratic-Republicans (Thomas Jefferson). The Federalists believed in a strong national government, while the Democratic-Republicans believed in greater local and state control of issues. The *Sentinel* joined the fray as a voice for the "Bucktails and Democratic."

Although the two presidents who signified the two parties were out of office by the time the *Sentinel* began publication, Davison leaped into the middle of the conflict, openly backing both Presidents Jackson and Van Buren.

The term "Bucktails," refers to a division in the state Democratic - Republican Party. Van Buren's supporters wore the tails of wild deer at a convention to demonstrate their opposition to fellow party member and governor, DeWitt Clinton, developer of the Erie Canal.

Joined later by his sons, Davison expanded his printing business by venturing into the publication of books. In 1842, after publishing the newspaper for 24 years, Davison sold the *Sentinel* while he continued publishing books and doing private printing. In addition to a math textbook, Davison published several editions of *Analysis of the Mineral Waters of Saratoga and Ballston; with practical remarks on their medical properties,* written by Dr. John H. Steel. This book had a wide circulation and added to the reputation of Saratoga. His company also published other thrillers by Saratogians including Esek Cowen and Nicholas Hill's 1839 four volume series *Cowen and Hill; Notes on Phillips' Evidence.* This was one of the first books that set the precedents for State Courts.

Davison was a man with economic vision. When the railroads started to be built in the 1830s, he invested in companies that were developing the local lines. The railroads in the mid 1800s were like the early internet; they tended to be numerous, small operations. In the case of the railroad companies, they often had the rights to connect only two or three hamlets. Gideon owned enough stock in the Saratoga and Whitehall Railroad that his son, John (595 Br), became its president. Railroads depended on customers, the seasonal nature of the tourist business and the heavy snows of winter resulted in most of the local rail lines Davison invested in being not particularly successful. Davison's railroads became profitable when the tracks were leased to Vanderbilt and the New York Central – Vanderbilt used to vacation in Saratoga each summer and Davison knew him personally.

In the 1800s the railroads were to communities what major highways are today – if one is in or near your community, it grows; if not, the community will stagnate. Vanderbilt's decision to have Saratoga on the main line between New York City and Montreal was a major contributor to Saratoga's growth in an era prior to the independence provided by of the automobile.

BROADWAY

465

Dr. Pearsall

Built in 1872, this was the home and office of Dr. Samuel Pearsall, the oldest of the three Pearsall brothers. Like most of the residences in this section of the village, this house was built to have a professional office in the lower floor and the family would live in the upper floors.

There were three Pearsall brothers, all of whom were doctors in the village at the same time. Samuel was a doctor of homeopathic medicine. John was a physician/surgeon (116 Cr) and Edward was a dentist (167 Sp). Their father was a successful farmer in Wilton. Samuel's son, William, the only male in the line, would become a physician in New York City.

In the 1870s several doctors in Saratoga were practicing homeopathic medicine. This more natural field of medicine was undergoing an upsurge; in part because people were looking for an alternative to the medical problems that had occurred during the recent Civil War. On the streets of every village were husbands, sons and neighbors who had come home from the war minus a limb or suffering from long-term illness. It appeared to some that the physician/surgeons had acted too quickly, and looking at some of the early war photographs where piles of limbs were next to a tent, one would have to agree. People were also justifiably concerned about the mortality rate of patients in military hospitals. The desire for homeopathic medicine may have been more out of lack of faith in physician/surgeons than a commitment based on science.

With an economy based in part on the perceived healing effects of the local mineral springs, one would have expected that homeopathic medicine would have been readily accepted in the village of Saratoga. According to Pearsall's biography in *Sylvester's* that was not the case. He cited the problems he had starting his practice because he had to overcome prejudices against non-surgical medicine.

Pearsall's problems achieving recognition would have been exacerbated by Dr. Allen, one of his fellow doctors of homeopathic medicine in the village. In 1875 Dr. Thomas Allen had a medical institute at the corner of Lafayette and Circular Streets. Several of Dr. Allen's patients, including some who were staying at his institute, died as the result of a smallpox breakout. Fearing his patients might go to other doctors, Dr. Allen began burying the dead at night in Greenridge Cemetery. The physician/surgeons brought him up on charges of violating the health laws. Dr. Allen's unsuccessful defense was that he could not tell the difference between chickenpox and smallpox. A defense of failure to diagnose one of the most feared diseases in the country had to hurt business for the other homeopathic physicians.

In several biographies throughout the 1890s Dr. Pearsall told of his continued success and expanding patient base. When banker railroad tycoon Jay Gould became ill in Saratoga, Dr. Pearsall was one of his attending physicians.

It was known that in addition to his home, Dr. Pearsall owned the building on Broadway to the left of his house. It was not until his death in the early 1900s that Dr. Samuel Pearsall's true financial status surfaced. When his son, William, tried to settle his father's estate it was discovered that Samuel was bankrupt. This may have been in part because of the declining value of real estate in Saratoga.

His son, William, practiced in New York City. He had no children and the Pearsall name, which had been so prevalent, disappeared from the village.

BROADWAY

489

VanNess

For several decades this house was owned by the VanNess family. The first VanNess resident was Anna, the widow of Joseph. She appears to have purchased the building because it provided the ability to have a commercial operation in the lowest level and a residence above. For the remainder of her life Anna would live in the upper floors.

About 1900 Anna's son, George, opened a grocery store in lowest level. The store was the principal market in this middle- class neighborhood. George did not live with his mother, having his own residence on Van Dam Street. Even after Anna died, George chose not to live above his store. He would, however, operate the grocery store for several decades.

While Anna VanNess was alive the upper two floors were one unit; however, when she died George converted the apartment that comprised the upper floors into two units.

VanNess grocery eventually experienced the fate of all small neighborhood stores losing out to the larger operations that began after the Second World War.

BROADWAY

491

Mingay

The century old drugstore on the corner of Broadway and Lake Avenue is named Menges and Curtis. It was originally named Mingay and Curtis; James Mingay being one of the original owners when it moved to its present site.

Born in England in 1844, when James was six his mother, four brothers and two sisters immigrated to the United States. His father, a cobbler, had preceded them establishing a residence and shop in Saratoga.

When the Southern troops fired on Fort Sumter, Mingay's brother, Henry, was working part-time at the *Saratogian* and as a runner for the telegraph office. Henry was the messenger selected to deliver to the newspaper the telegram announcing the beginning of the war. Henry immediately resigned from both positions to enlist for the Union (Henry lived to be over 100 and was drawn as an old civil war soldier in a cartoon by Disney).

In 1857 at the age of 13 James stopped attending school (not that young for the period) and started working as a clerk in Hill & Company a local drugstore. When the Civil War first broke out James was too young to enlist so he had to wait until he was 18. In

August of 1862 he enlisted as a sergeant in the 115th New York (Saratoga's other company). In 1864 he was transferred from the Volunteers into the United States Army where he served as a hospital steward. He was discharged with the rank of sergeant. When the war ended James returned to Saratoga where he worked in a drugstore owned by Frank Wolcott. In 1869, James bought out Wolcott and moved his store to its present location. While working as a druggist Mingay invested extensively in real estate. He remained in the drugstore until 1889 when he sold his interest to Frederic Menges. At the age of 45 James Mingay retired (or at least stopped going to work).

Mingay married Louise Hill of Malta in 1873. Her family had a deep history in the country. In 1901 she was made a regent in the DAR. The couple had no children.

In 1890 G. F. Harvey Co. (see) was incorporated. With the money from the sale of his store Mingay was in a position to invest significant funds in Harvey's venture. His stock holdings were sufficient enough that he was made secretary and a director of the new drug company. He was also a director of the Adirondack Trust Company and the Citizen's Bank. He and Edgar Brackett (605 Br) were close personal friends and they shared many of the same investments.

In 1894 Mingay sold this house and moved into all the floors that constitute the north quarter of the Pardue Block (now the Algonquin). He and his wife lived in the north section and G. F. Harvey, his wife and daughter lived in the south quarter. He would later build the house at 100 Lake Avenue. The story of that part of his life, including his around the world trip in which he visited almost every country in the world at the time, will be told with that house.

Since he was retired, Mingay had time to devote to community service; especially his favorite, the Masonic Order. One of the tasks he voluntarily undertook was to write the history of the local Masonic Order for the group's centennial in 1908.

BROADWAY

493

Dr. Whiting
Dr. Reynolds

The first two owners of this house were both physicians who, like others on the street, lived in the upper floors and used the below ground level door as an entrance to their professional office. The two doctors shared two rather unusual characteristics. They both were married, yet died without having any children and they both died as the result of a seizure they experienced while getting out of their carriage. The next owner was not until after the automobile so he escaped the curse.

Dr. Lewis Whiting and his wife, Diantha, moved to Saratoga from Massachusetts in 1843. After living very comfortably for several years in a residential hotel, they elected to have this house built. Whiting was a member of Congregational Church serving on its original board. A public servant, for three years Whiting was a member of the board of education including serving as its president in his last year, 1871-72. Like many of his neighbors Whiting was an active Mason; at one time he even provided the group with space for a meeting hall. He, along with several other men who lived on Broadway, created a short-lived organization named the Saratoga Musical Association. This organization was devoted to the advancement of the appreciation of music providing concerts and other performances for the public. Whiting was also a director of Congress Spring which means he was a part owner.

In 1882, sixty-seven year old Whiting had a seizure while getting out of his carriage and died almost immediately. After he died his wife moved out of the area.

The second owner was Dr. Tabor Reynolds, who like Whiting used it for both a home and an office. Reynolds was born, raised, and lived most of his life in the Town of Wilton. After graduating from Albany Medical College, he joined his father and brother in the practice of medicine in his home town. In addition to being a physician Reynolds was active in politics, serving as the superintendent of the town's schools (an elected office), town supervisor and state assemblyman. When the Civil War broke out Reynolds was forty years old. He did not serve in the war but took an active role supporting the troops. As Wilton Town Supervisor, his responsibilities included to serve as county legislator, in which capacity he was actively involved in recruiting volunteers for the 77th New York; the Saratoga Company. Since the local troops were primarily in one company, he took an active part in insuring that their needs for such things as blankets, tents and even clothing were provided.

When the Civil War was over many public offices went to those who served. Reynolds' respect within the region was demonstrated by his being elected sheriff in 1867. When it was time to run for re-election in 1870, Reynolds did not run; however, he was the assemblyman from 1867-71 (he held two office as the same time). His brother, who was also his partner, died that year. His wife was very ill so Reynolds gave up politics and focused on his medical practice. His wife died in 1874, but by that time Reynolds no longer sought public office.

Reynolds continued to practice medicine literally until the day he died. He had a heart attack getting out of his carriage after treating a patient. Reynolds was 80 years old.

BROADWAY

495

Dr. Murray

Born in 1850 in Luzerne, Warren County, Dr. Byron Murray was the son of a doctor.

Considered an adolescent today, at thirteen Murray, without his family, moved to Michigan where he worked as a clerk in a drug store. By the time he was twenty (1870) he entered the University of Michigan first in the literary department but transferred to the school of medicine, graduating in 1876.

After graduation he had practiced medicine in several places including Indiana, the Town of Wilton where he served on the board of Supervisors, and New York City. In 1887 he settled in Saratoga. He and his wife, Iva, had one son, Leon, who died when he was ten. The son's death coincided with Murray's move to New York City.

In 1900 his mother was living with him at this address, which is interesting, since he left home "to find his own way" when he was thirteen.

Murray was less active than most of his neighbors only claiming a membership in the Odd Fellows. Iva, his wife, died in 1913. He lived until 1933, dying at the age of 83.

This house may be hard to see, since it has been combined with the building next to it to create a hotel.

BROADWAY

505

Durkee

One of Saratoga's earliest politicians, Judge Nicholas Doe had this house built around 1843, making him one of Chancellor Walworth's nearest neighbors. Born in New York City, educated at Phillips Exeter Academy, Doe was a county judge, assemblyman, and congressman; all positions he held before building this house. Doe's wife lived in the house until her death in 1864.

There are unusual ways people demonstrate their strength. Paoli Durkee, the second owner died Feb. 4, 1880 at the age 74, exactly two weeks before he had been a pall bearer at a friend's funeral. He was only bedridden for his last two days. Born in Vermont, Paoli graduated from the University of Vermont and had honorary degrees from Middlebury College. He moved to Saratoga in 1849 to open a private academy for boys in what had been Washington Hall on North Broadway. He would maintain the school until 1858 when he opened a stationery and bookstore.

Durkee's store, on the corner of Broadway and Spring Street, was in a prime location. The Grand Union Hotel and Congress Hall were both directly across the street; the United States Hotel was only a half block away. His store was directly in line between two of these hotels and the springs. With everyone expected to write to family and friends each day while they were in Saratoga, Durkee's location was where the action was each morning.

Paoli was committed to education in Saratoga serving on the board of Temple Grove (a private school) and President of the Board of Education 1872-73. In an event that would be unheard of today, Paoli was the moderator at the first adult spelling bee in the village. When Paoli and his wife died they left the house to their only son, Cornelius.

Cornelius is known today for the volumes of history that he wrote. The books are rich in tales of early Saratoga documenting dates and names.

Cornelius was also a member of Saratoga's first baseball team. The team was an eclectic with sons of some of the wealthiest men in town playing beside butchers and liverymen. The team which called itself the Hay Makers, was formed in reaction to the sudden national growth of the sport before the Civil War. When they decided to form a team none of the players had ever even seen a game. So unsophisticated were the team members that they had to send to the Spaulding company in New York City for bats, balls, and rule books (note: no mention is made of gloves). They laid out the first field based on a drawing in the rule book. During practice, after each play they would check the books to see if they had followed the rules. Unlike the league play today, the local boys had to purchase their own shirts, pants and belts. Eventually they were bold enough to challenge a club from Ballston Spa made up of men who worked in the tannery. They soon learned their egos were better than their play. Cornelius described the outcome: "We found our outfield was weak and started making changes … we also worked on our base running." In short, they lost.

As a young man Cornelius Durkee was a character. With a group of five other young Saratogians, he decided that they should set out on a boat trip from Schuylerville to Montreal. Using an early steam ship they traveled through the canal then down Lake Champlain sleeping on the boat at night. Despite leaks in the wooden hull and one storm the group reached Montreal where they slept in hotels. Durkee enjoy the excursion; however, there is no record of how they got the boat back.

In 1883 he and group of friends decided to open the first toboggan slide called the Woodlawn Park Toboggan Club. They purchased four toboggans from Montreal. The club would be replaced by the one at the Gen Mitchell, which is often depicted in drawings.

Cornelius was a member of Nights Templar; a Mason and the secretary of the Saratoga Club (an all male social club). He worked in his father's store then for many years he was a freight agent for the Delaware & Hudson RR. He married Josephine Davison the daughter of Gideon Davison (417 Br) and the older sister of John Davison (509 Br).

Unless someone records why they take on a project others can only speculate as to the reasons. There is no record of why Durkee decided to become a local historian. It may have been because he and his wife had no children. It may have been because he had grown up in the village and worked as a freight agent putting him a position where he literally knew everyone. It may have been because he was concerned about his own legacy. Whatever the reason Cornelius Durkee's writings would become one of the best sources of information about Saratoga and the people who he lived among.

BROADWAY

509

Davison

This house was built as the residence of John Davison, the eldest son of Gideon Davison (425 Br). John married Sarah Walworth, the daughter of Chancellor Walworth (see). The house would have been on property that was originally part of the Walworth estate, Pine Grove. Conveniently this residence was also just down the street from his parents' home (425). Later in her life, John's older sister married Cornelius Durkee, who lived immediately next door (505 Br). John and Sarah's son, Charles, would live at 173 Caroline Street and would become an international arbitrator for President Cleveland. This second generation Saratoga family is a prime example of how much the early families were intertwined.

John Davison had multiple careers. Before he was trained as a printer by his father he worked as a clerk/manager in the dry goods store owned by Rockwell Putnam. In 1838 he was appointed Register of the Chancellery under his father-in-law. Along with his father, John invested in the early railroads eventually assuming the duties of President of the Saratoga and Whitehall RR. Under Vanderbilt's heavy hand the railroad became part of the Delaware and Hudson. After the merger, John returned to the printing business.

The house was later owned by Harry Leonard who was involved in a major insurance company. Still later the house was owned by designer Herbert Waring.

BROADWAY

511

Dr. Moriarata

This office/residence was designed by Breeze and lived in by Dr. Douglas Moriarta a successful physician. Dr. Moriarta, perhaps more than any other professional person in town at the time, could testify that public service is all too often a thankless waste of time that can tarnish a person's reputation forever.

The year the scandal exploded in the newspaper was 1905; however, most of the incidents occurred in previous years. It was a period when, because companies were bottling the carbon dioxide gas, the mineral springs were barely perking; the grand hotels were showing their age; and the state government was pushing enforcement of the gambling laws. All these resulted in Saratoga experiencing a serious economic decline. The village's answer was the same as most communities; turn frustration into anger then direct it against each other.

Dr. Moriarta was serving on the village's Street, Water and Sewer Commission; a position for which there was no salary. In 1905, Moriarta and another board member were charged with official misconduct the allegations that started the issues were:

• That pages from the old account books were torn out (an

issue not in dispute; however the reason was)

- That Dr. Moriarta had abused his power by disciplining an employee (the person in question had been suspended for 15 days without pay)
- That Dr. Moriarta had used village employees to perform work at his personal property (a fact not in dispute the issue was who paid the people the doctor or did the village).
- That Dr. Moriarta influenced the awarding of contracts (an issue very much in contention).
- That Dr. Moriarta was aware that village employees were charging residents a premium for the privilege of tapping into the village's water supply and keeping the premium.
- That in his professional capacity Dr. Moriarta received money for treating village employees in excess of what the village officials had approved (an issue subject to debate).
- That the doctor or the superintendent he supervised had received "draw downs" (kickbacks) for granting contracts to local companies.

The principle record of what occurred is found in the newspapers of the day. Exactly what happened will never be determined. In part the truth is hidden because reporters did not have the space to record all the testimony, forcing them to choose what to include in their accounts. The reporters' screening automatically placed a bias on the accounts.

Dr. Moriarta was born, raised, and schooled in politics in Saratoga. Giving him the benefit of the doubt, one would assume that since Dr. Moriarta was a native son he may have naively assumed that what was occurring within his department was acceptable. He may also have assumed that there was nothing improper with his hiring for personal work, people he was responsible for as a public official.

Although Dr. Moriarta was not paid for his service on the Street, Sewer and Water Commission, he was receiving a stipend from the village of "$700 or $800" for being the village health official (the doctor was making sufficient money, that he was not sure how much he received from the village). For the reader's perspective the superintendent of the water works was receiving $60 a month for a full time (44 hour a week) position.

Formal charges were brought before the village trustees by a group of concerned citizens referred to as the Committee of Fifteen.

This group was comprised of many of the people on North Broadway including; French, Hewitt, and Gage. There were also representatives from other parts of the village; including the Milligans (102 Cr).

The village trustees conducted a hearing into the charges, similar to what would probably be conducted today before a grand jury. Having the hearing before trustees, however, allowed for the potential for a very different outcome than may have happened before a more neutral jury. First the testimony as to whether to initiate formal charges was taken in public (grand jury testimony is behind closed doors). Second, trustees are elected officials who might be motivated by either the political outcome or their connections to the people involved. At the hearing, Dr. Moriarta and Annis, the other commissioner under investigation, were defended by the most political person in the village, Senator Brackett (605 Br).

The hearings took several days with some trustees missing some or all of the testimony. One trustee even resigned his office during the investigation; it is not clear if his resignation was to avoid taking part in the vote. A second trustee had to excuse himself because of a potential conflict of interest with Dr. Moriarta.

After the testimony of many people including village employees, contractors and Dr. Moriarta, the trustees went into executive session to vote on the charges. Out of the public eye, and the reporters' ability to hear, meant that the discussions during the deliberations have been lost. The final votes of the trustees are recorded by name.

The outcome
Moriarta- Annis Exonerated of Taxpayers Charges.

The headlines in the *Saratogian* demonstrated once again America's misunderstanding of its own judicial system. In America there are two possible verdicts; guilty or not-guilty. A not-guilty verdict does not mean the person was innocent, it only means that there was not evidence beyond a reasonable doubt. Some European counties do have a verdict of innocent which is when the evidence shows that the person did not commit the act.

To have the commissioners removed from office and legal charges brought required at least seven affirmative votes. With one open seat on the board of trustees and an additional member disqualified because of a conflict of interest, reaching the seventh vote was made difficult since it meant that seven out of eleven votes was required. Almost all the charges against Moriarta resulted in a vote of six to five; with the majority feeling that removal from office and legal action was appropriate. The problem was that what was required was a majority vote of the entire board not a vote of the majority present. The president of the board put forward an excellent conclusion; "The commissioners (Moriarta and Annis) have been found guilty of the charges but they may not be removed from office."

Dr. Moriarta may have survived the assault but the anguish of having one's name carried in the newspapers for charges such as these is something one never gets over.

It should be noted that two of the charges against Annis failed to garner even a single vote for conviction. All seven charges against Dr. Moriarta resulted in at least five votes for conviction. Annis would later file suit against the Committee of Fifteen for slander and defamation of character – but that is another story to be told when Annis' house is covered.

Dr. Moriarta would return to the practice of medicine and leave politics for those who enjoy the limelight.

There is confusion between two of Saratoga's old names, Moriarta and Moriarty. To add to the confusion the Moriarta brothers were the children of Moriarty. For some unexplained reason the sons took a different name than their father.

BROADWAY

513

Dr. Varney

For many years this small, sheltered building was the combination home and office of Dr. Miles Varney. Miles was from a family with very deep roots in the region. Born in Luzerne, New York, his parents provided him with the best education possible. His father was a millwright yet arranged for Miles to attend Fort Edward Collegiate Institute, Oakwood Academy, and the University of Vermont.

Starting in with a practice in South Glens Falls, by 1894 Varney moved to Saratoga where he was a general practitioner. From its beginning, Varney was associated with Saratoga Hospital. He was listed as a surgeon with a general practice. In addition to his work for the hospital he was a physician for the railroad and several insurance companies.

One unusual distinction of Dr. Varney's was his interest in the total life span of his patients. He was one of the first physicians in the village to list "maternity" as a specialty. At the same time he was the county's corner. He saw his patients both ways.

In addition to being a member of many medical societies, like many of his neighbors, Dr. Varney was a Mason, a member of Knights Templar, and a member of the YMCA.

In his last year of college (1988), Dr. Varney married Sadie Austin of Burlington. They had no children.

Walworth
When there is too much in a name

There is one family name that was a fixture on Broadway for 120 years and has since disappeared from Saratoga's directories. The family's house is also gone so, unlike other families in this book, the story can not be associated with a specific building. While residing in his house on Broadway, the patriarch entertained at least three presidents; a presidential candidate; numerous congressmen; statesmen; senators; men in the clergy (including the first American Cardinal); professors; judges, including a US Supreme Court Justice; authors and musicians. The list of those he entertained in his own house could only be rivaled by Yaddo.

A man of such stature, by his very nature, sends waves of energy not only through the social world of a community but also through his own family. Of his four daughters three would reach adulthood. One would marry a minister, a second the president of a railroad; the third would we be widowed young. He would have two sons; both would become published authors. One son would become a priest, the other would be murdered. His only daughter-in-law would form a national society the power of which is still felt today. Of the three granddaughters who bore the family name, one would be a heroine; another, an author; the third a nun. As a father and mentor he could best be described as casting an intense shadow in which all were expected to grow but few could truly flourish.

As a sign of respect, Reuben Hyde Walworth was and is referred to as Chancellor. It was a title he earned as the last Chancellor of the Court of Errors (position abolished by an amendment to the State Constitution in 1847).

Born in Connecticut to a family with deep American roots and political roots in Europe, Chancellor Walworth's father had been a major in the Revolutionary War. While still a boy the family moved to a farm in Eastern New York State along the Vermont border. Like most farm children the Chancellor was educated at the small public school. At seventeen he moved to Troy where he taught school and read for the law. One of the lawyers he studied under was the State's Attorney for the Northern District. It was while reading for the law that the future Chancellor would become familiar with Plattsburgh.

His early connection with a State's Attorney would allow his legal skills to be recognized at an early age. At twenty-two Walworth was admitted to the bar. At about the same time he chose to seek his fortunes by moving north of the Adirondacks.

Arriving in Plattsburgh in 1810, Walworth had inadvertently placed himself in the right place at the right time. Two years later the War of 1812 would break out and Plattsburgh would play a significant role in stopping the British's 1814 advance up Lake Champlain. With the rank of major, Walworth served with distinction and was the adjutant to the Major General in charge of the American army in the region.

In 1821 Walworth was elected to the United States Congress. His term as a legislator ended in 1823 at which time he became a Circuit Court Judge for the State. Circuit Judges tended to dislike their positions because it meant being away from family and friends for extended periods; staying in uncertain surroundings; traveling on back roads in uncomfortable vehicles; and being confronted by an assortment of lawyers and citizens. Walworth used the appointment as a catalyst to move from Plattsburgh to Saratoga where he purchased a house known as Pine Grove. The house was similar in design to 1 Franklin Square without the pillars or stone. The main body of the house was set between two side wings. The house was demolished in the 1950s and has been replaced by a gas station – not all choices are good ones.

The circuit court provided Walworth with a chance to gain a reputation for fairness. In 1828, Walworth was rewarded with a major promotion when he was appointed Chancellor of the Court of Errors. Only forty, he was young for such an important position. As Chancellor he did not hear cases, rather, he reviewed decisions made by other judges. There is no equivalent position in the court system today; although it would be roughly equivalent to the Chief Justice of a States Supreme Court without having to deal with the other associate justices. He would hold the position of Chancellor for twenty years and use the title for the rest of his life. He revamped the court, establishing procedures that were still followed by subsequent courts for many decades.

Since the position of Chancellor involved cases from across the state rather than one region, Walworth moved his family to Albany so he would hear appeals in the Capitol of the state; he retained Pine Grove as a seasonal retreat. After five years (1833) Walworth realized that he was the court and moved his family back to Saratoga. For the next fifteen year appeals were heard in one of the rooms in his house.

One of the cases the Chancellor reviewed included arguments by Daniel Webster. Knowing the great orator was in town, people gathered outside the Chancellor's office to listen to Webster speak. There were so many people that the Chancellor moved the court from his house to the building that still stands on the corner of Woodlawn and Church Street.

The Court of Appeals replaced the Chancellor of the Court of Errors. It is interesting to note that for at least the first fifty years after the change, the Court of Appeals met each May and June at the Walton Hotel in Saratoga. This choice appears to have been a remnant from Walworth's court being held in Saratoga.

In 1844, President Tyler nominated Walworth to fill an open position on the United States Supreme Court. There are three reasons given for why Walworth was not selected. One holds that Henry Clay opposed his appointment (very logical). A second was that there was a political disagreement within the New York State machine (logical). The third reason reported was that President Tyler was mistaken about one of Walworth's associations (unlikely). The reason President Tyler withdrew his nomination of Walworth was probably a little of each.

In 1848 the Chancellor was nominated for governor by the National Democracy Party. He was defeated.

Walworth was one of those people considered a character in his own community. Tall, considered handsome, he worked incredibly long and late hours. Many people noted that he was still sitting at his desk working on court business well into the night. When the style changed to coats with sleeves replacing cloaks, Walworth was unimpressed and continued to wear his outdated capes until he died. However, it could not be said that he did not care about appearances; when he retired he maintained his own flower gardens, which were considered among the finest in the village.

The Chancellor was a social person. Each day he would peruse the column of the newspaper that told who had arrived at each hotel (such a column was a regular feature). If he recognized a name he would be sure to stop and pay the person a courtesy visit. He was equally attuned to his own neighbors. Even as an old man, each New Year's Day he would be among the first to attend each open house in the village.

At his eulogy one of the young lawyers pointed out that what accomplishments he had made were through his own diligence. Walworth had not been born to a family with wealth or influence, nor was he afforded a classical education. He was considered by his peers as knowledgeable but not overly brilliant. As a judge he was considered fair, consistent, and open to thoughtful arguments. He was a man noted for his logic, integrity and kindness.

The Chancellor was a man of strong convictions and a certain duality of message. He believed in the power of government to change people's lives and to ensure personal liberty. The Chancellor believed states guaranteed personal rights by ensuring justice. The duality is shown in his opposition to alcohol. He was the president of the National Temperance Association, which believed the government should stop the sale of alcohol, in effect stopping a personal liberty, a position he purported to support.

After he retired from the bench the Chancellor became interested in genealogy tracing his mother's family. The published work that he generated was over 1200 pages.

The Chancellor was an active member of the Masons and of the Knights Templar; both of which sent large contingents to his funeral.

The Chancellor's first wife was Maria Ketchum Avery. A woman of her time, Maria was considered to be the perfect wife for a man of stature. Active in her church and in pursuing causes for those less fortunate, she was also the core around which the family developed. The Chancellor and Maria had four daughters and two sons. The sons will be discussed later. The daughters were Sarah, who became Mrs. John Davison (509 Br); Mary, who became Mrs. Edgar Jenkins (1812 – 75) and moved back into the family house upon the death of her mother; Eliza, who married the Reverend Dr. E. T. Backus, a minister from Schenectady; the fourth daughter, Frances, died at age 5. Maria died in 1847, the year before her husband lost his position as Chancellor and the race for Governor.

Sarah Smith Harden, the Chancellor's second wife, had deep roots in the Midwest (Kentucky and Illinois). She was the widow of Col. John Harden who, as a Congressman, also led a local militia. He died in the Battle of Buena Vista in the Mexican War. She outlived the Chancellor, remaining at Pine Grove until her own death in 1874.

When Sarah and the Chancellor married in 1851, she brought to Pine Grove her own three children. One of her sons, Martin Harden, would graduate from West Point in 1859 and serve in the Union Army. During the war he rose in rank from lieutenant to general assuming command of the Illinois Volunteers. He lost his left arm in the Second Battle of Bull Run but continued to serve until the end of the war. Her second son, Lemuel, served in the Confederate

Army in a unit referred to as Mosby's Raiders. After the war Lemuel would move to New York City becoming a lawyer and journalist.

It is in his own sons that the duality of the father's personality can be seen. The Chancellor's sons were Clarence (b. 1820) and Mansfield Tracy (b. 1830). Both sons would graduate from Union College; both would become lawyers; and both would be published authors.

Clarence only practiced law for one year then began the study of theology. Within a few years he converted to Catholicism moving to Belgium where he taught at the College at Wittemberg. This is the same place where he became an ordained priest. The late 1840s and 1850s were a period of missionary work by Catholic priests in Protestant countries. Clarence worked as a missionary first in England then for 15 years in the United States. In 1865 he would give up missionary work for reported health reasons. He returned to New York State assuming the leadership of St. Mary's Church in Albany. Among his conversions would be several of his sister-in-law's children.

Clarence is attributed with both original writing and translations. Many of the translations are of hymns from German to English. His published works include several that are religious: *The Gentle Skeptic*, and *The Oxford Movement in America or Glimpses of Life in an Anglican Seminary*.

It is his non-theological book that raises interest. Like his own father, Father Clarence in his later life became interested in his family's history in this country. That may in part be the result of his realizing that he was the last male Walworth and being a priest the family name would cease to exist upon his death. In 1897 he published *The Walworths of America comprising five chapters on Family History with additional chapters on Genealogy*. This book was a continuation of his father's work of four decades previous.

While Clarence gave up earthly law for the advancement of religious principles, his brother, Mansfield, gave up law for literature. After graduating from Union College (1847) and Albany Law School (1852), Mansfield Tracy Walworth wrote the book *Mission of Death* (1853). In 1855 he was admitted to the bar and practiced law for a period while continuing to write. He would eventually devote his efforts completely to writing, earning his income both from magazines and full length novels.

Mansfield was 21 and attending Albany Law School when his father remarried. He was apparently taken by his stepsister, 19 year-old Ellen Hardin, who he soon married. The two would have six children, two boys and four girls. A large part of Mansfield's problems may have been that he married a woman as strong as his father. As he could not measure up to his father, time would show that Mansfield had problems standing next to his wife.

Unlike his stepbrothers, Mansfield would not serve during the Civil War choosing instead to take Ellen and their children to her former home in Kentucky. Kentucky, as a border state, was a place where residents were kept under close scrutiny. In 1862 Mansfield found himself in trouble with the Union Army and was arrested for being a southern spy. He had become "fascinated" with a widow named Morris with some claims that they had become "peculiarly intimate." He was arrested when his luggage was searched and he was found to be carrying pistols, powder, and a bowie knife. Any one of these contraband items would have been grounds to place a man in an internment camp for years. It took all of his father's influence to keep Mansfield out of prison. The rift that developed between father and son was deep. It is not surprising that Mansfield and his family did not return to Saratoga to live until after his father's death.

While Clarence Walworth embraced the humble work of the church, Mansfield continued to try his hand in the more egotistical literary circles. During his lifetime Mansfield published a total of seven novels. After his death, three other works would be printed based on his manuscripts. One of the posthumous books was the *Life of Chancellor Livingston*, his only non-fiction work.

Ellen Hardin Walworth was a force, the equal of her father-in-law. Born a hundred years later she would have been at least a senator. During her lifetime, Ellen experienced: her father being killed as a hero in the Mexican American War; her husband being disgraced when he was arrested for being a spy; her husband being murdered; one of her sons would be convicted of murder; one of her daughters would die from typhoid she contracted serving others; another daughter would become a nun; her second son would be weak and unable to handle the trials of life; and the death of three of her six children.

She would rise above her tribulations and write two books, and numerous magazine articles. She would become one of the founding members of the Daughters of the American Revolution; and she would be on the committee to fund the Saratoga Monument Association. She started a girls' boarding school; became a member of the board of education (before women had suffrage); and during the Spanish American War she was the Director General of the Women's National Relief Association.

The two books she wrote were *The Battles of Saratoga 1777: the Saratoga Monument Association* and *The Battle of Saratoga: Battle Ground Visitors' Guide.*

Mansfield's temperament may have rendered him ill-suited for marriage. Within the first years of his marriage he began engaging in "countless whims." Whether the fault was his or not, the marriage of Ellen and Mansfield could be described in many terms; however, those terms would almost all be negative. If not physically abusive, Mansfield was at the very least verbally cruel. He added to his infamous reputation by not restricting his abuse to Ellen but inflicting his venom on his children as well.

The situation between Mansfield and his wife deteriorated to a point that when the Chancellor died in 1866, he left Mansfield's portion of the estate in a trust rather than allowing his son access to the money. Mansfield was many things; patience was not one of them. Tying up the money he felt was his only angered him more.

By 1870, Ellen felt it was essential that she leave her husband and return to her mother's home in Saratoga. To help support her family Ellen opened a girls' school at Pine Grove.

Mansfield moved to New York City to pursue his literary ambitions and whims. Although he earned a living from his writings, Mansfield was not considered to have true talent. In one of his last works Mansfield told the story of a dysfunctional family, which many readers considered to be an intimate tale about his own marriage. Frustrated Mansfield had taken to writing Ellen threatening letters. The last letter he wrote said in part: "I will kill your boys, and defeat the ___ scoundrel in his grave (the Chancellor), and cut off his ___ name forever." He added, "You may be certain that, sooner or later, I will fulfill my promise."

The Walworth Tragedy

On Monday morning, June 2, 1873, nineteen year-old Frank Walworth, oldest son of Mansfield and Ellen, walked the two blocks from Pine Grove to the railroad station. There he boarded a south bound train to New York City. Knowing words might make him rethink his mission, he had deliberately not said goodbye to any of his family.

Once in New York City, Frank checked into the Sturtevant House. He refreshed himself by taking a bath then went to the house where his father boarded. Finding that his father was out, Frank left the following note, "I want to try and settle some family matters. Call at the Sturtevant House in an hour or two. If I am not there I will leave word at the office."

A man who tried to control all things, Mansfield did not arrive at the time requested. In fact he did not come to his son's hotel at all that evening.

Frank waited in the room as hour after hour passed. He did not sleep at all that night.

The difference in the size of Mansfield and Frank is noteworthy. Mansfield was a large stocky man, capable of exerting considerable physical force. Frank was built almost the exact opposite. He would have to be described as thin, even compared to his counterparts of the time. Frank also suffered from severe epilepsy.

At 6:15 in the morning Mansfield finally showed up at the Sturtevant House where he asked at the desk for his son's room. Not being sure a guest would be welcome at such an early hour, a bellhop escorted Mansfield to his son's room. There was a debate about how long it was after Mansfield entered the room until the time the first shot was fired. The bellhop maintained it was only moments; Frank insisted that he and his father had time to talk.

The following paragraphs are based on what Frank related to the arresting officers:

Mansfield entered his son's room taking a seat in a chair near the window. Frank told his father that he "must promise me (that you will) not make any more of the threats against mother and to cease writing insulting letters to her."

Frank went on to characterize his father's response as a sneering, "I suppose I'll promise."

The report Frank gave of what followed shows the level to which the family's relationships had digressed and that trust was gone. With a pistol in hand Frank went on, "You have lied to my mother and myself so often that I can hardly believe you now."

Frank claimed that his father then reached into his own pocket. Assuming his father was planning to draw a pistol, Frank opened fire shooting four shots; three hit their mark.

Frank stood up and walked out of the room. A guest in the next room heard the shots and went out into the hall to investigate. He saw Frank walking calmly down the hall. When the other guest reached the door to Frank's room he found it was slightly ajar. He pushed the door open and saw Mansfield's body lying on the floor in a puddle of blood.

Frank walked calmly down the stairs and up to the front desk of the hotel. He wrote out a telegram then asked for directions to the nearest police station. The telegram was addressed to his uncle, Martin Hardin (the one who lost his arm in the war), which read: "I have shot and killed father."

Given directions to the local precinct, Frank exited the hotel. When Frank reached the police station he surrendered himself to the desk sergeant.

Even in a time when justice was swift, the velocity of the trial of Frank Walworth was nearly record setting. The shooting took place on June 3, 1873 and the trial was over on July 2 of the same year. Despite the efforts of some of the best lawyers in the country, including Saratogian, William A. Beach, Frank Walworth was convicted of second degree murder. The judge, in a letter to the governor, noted that the conviction was correct but suggested that circumstances dictated that a pardon should be granted at some time in the future.

Frank was sent to prison first at Sing Sing; later to Auburn. His mother immediately began working tirelessly for his release. When Frank was at Auburn, Ellen Hardin Walworth was able to get him classified as insane and assigned to a detention center outside the prison walls. He was in what could be characterized as a home with four other inmates; one of whom was Henrietta Robinson (*Curse of the Veiled Murderess*). Motivated by the pressure he was receiving on behalf of both Frank Walworth and Henrietta Robinson, at one point Governor Robinson took the time to visit the Auburn center.

In August of 1877, the governor pardoned Frank but not Henrietta. Governor Robinson issued a long and well reasoned statement justifying his action. Basically he had listened to experts on the case, including the presiding judge at the trial, and people who knew Frank and Mansfield.

After four years in prison Frank was released into his mother's care. His health had declined and rumors of a trip to Europe were dismissed because he was too weak.

Six years later, 1883, the Walworths and their Kentucky connection would be reinforced by the marriage of Frank to Corinne Bramlette, the daughter of the man who had been governor of Kentucky during the Civil War. Three years later in 1886, they had a daughter, Clara, named in honor of one of Frank's sisters. The same year Frank died suddenly of pneumonia. His widow, Corinne, and daughter, Clara, would remain at Pine Grove.

Ellen and Mansfield's other children were also an interesting group. Their daughter Mary died before her second birthday.

Ellen, called Nellie, was named for her mother. In the 1880s she went on a world tour with her paternal uncle, Father Clarence. Upon her return she wrote the book *An Old World as Seen Through Young Eyes: or travels around the world*. She would also write, *The Life and Times of Kateri Tekakwitha: the Lily of the Mohawks*. This was the story of the first Native American woman to become a saint. Ellen never married.

Another daughter, Clara Walworth, became a nun of the order of the Sacred Heart. She lived in a convent in Albany.

The third daughter was Reubena Hyde Walworth, called Ruby. She was named after her grandfather the Chancellor and was equally as strong.

"If I can not fight I can nurse."

When the Spanish American War broke out in 1898, many men from Saratoga enlisted. The only surviving male Walworth was Tracy Mansfield, who considered himself too old for service. His younger sister Reubena announced that it was a Walworth family tradition to serve so she planned to become a nurse to treat the soldiers.

Ruby resigned her position as a teacher in a private girls' school to serve in the nurses' corps. She was one of the 1,000 women who were selected. When typhoid fever broke out at several camps she volunteered to help. By her own choice she served in the detention hospital on Montauk Point. She was the only female nurse assigned to that hospital. Bent on a mission to assist, and over her mother's objections, Ruby volunteered to be locked in the contagious ward. She was fully aware that she might never come out. Just as the outbreak among the men was coming to conclusion, she caught the fever. She rallied temporarily and was able to return to Saratoga. Her fever started again and Ruby died in December 1898 at the age of 31. Reubena's two surviving sisters and her brother had all converted to Catholicism. Upset about her failure to convert the three did not attend their sister's funeral.

Tracy Mansfield became a doctor but had a very limited practice. He, like his brother, was closely attached to his mother. When Ellen died he never fully recovered; in 1928 he took his own life.

Frank's wife, Corinne, never remarried living in Pine Grove until her death in 1937. Her daughter, Clara, the last of the Walworths, lived in Pine Gove until her death in 1952. She, like all her aunts, never married.

One floor of the museum in the Casino is dedicated to the Walworth family.

There are families where the dynamic nature of the parents overwhelms their children.

A Little About A Lot

It's all about People

A series of books on the houses of Saratoga could have taken several directions. The books could have been on architecture; someone suggested an in-depth history of a few of the houses; or even the relationship between a society and the houses it constructs. There was already a book on the architecture. There are several books that explore the history of Saratoga. There are even books on the society during the Victorian Era. To do another book along any of these lines was unnecessary.

The decision was made to write a series of books that was very different. This series is an attempt to tell the story of a city based on the families who built it. If the series is successful, and finished as planned, the end result will be a brief history of these beautiful houses based on the families that either built or lived in them for a long period of time. To contain the length of the books, the idea is to limit the story of each house to one family, understanding that there would be occasions where it will be important to tell of a second or even more residents.

The choice was made tell the story of one of the earliest families; that way I was less likely to anger those living in the houses today. In the case of a few of the oldest houses the task of finding the history of the family that built it was often too difficult, so the story is of a family that lived in the house between 1870 and 1910 – that makes the residents contemporaries of the others in the book.

A series about people but history matters

The people who have part of their story told here are those who lived in the houses on some of the older streets in the city. These are the people and families who directly influenced and impacted Saratoga up to at least the 1920s. In their own ways these are the people who built and rebuilt the city. There is a reason for focusing on people. To the author, history is the outcome that resulted from the interaction of the personalities involved in an event. In effect history is a drama based on the interactions between and the separations of people. These interpersonal dramas occurred because of the people's values, aspirations, and suffering; thus gambling, and the future of the springs both help build the city and at times divided its inhabitants.

This is a series about people; however, to understand how some of the characters interacted there occasionally needs to be an understanding of certain experiences and events. The question of where in the book to relate some of the more significant situations in the history of the village was considered at length. The first choice was to tell the situations just before the first home where it came into play. That solution would have been predicated on the assumption that readers read the book from beginning to end – and in reality the book was never meant to be read in the order it was laid out. The logical option was to group these pages. Grouping them raised the question: where in the book should they be placed? Pages at the beginning are skipped, pages at the end are considered peripheral, so they were placed in the relative middle so readers could quickly find the information.

Parameters for the books

From the conception of the idea of writing these books there were parameters. The primary requirement was that all the houses included in each volume be set up as self-guided walking tour. That meant that houses on a given street would be discussed together; in effect the reader would see neighbors as they related to each other. The second requirement was that the books be manageable while walking. That meant that each book should be 6 x 9 inches, and be about 200 pages. *Third, that the picture of each house should be with the text about the family - it is difficult to keep track while flipping back and forth.*

Additionally
1. This series is being written to be *enjoyable* reading. No matter how factual or accurate, a book that is not enjoyed is rarely read.
2. To cover as many houses as possible, the story of each of the "Great Ladies" would be held to one or two pages. It turned out that some houses had very special families and required additional space.
3. Special pages such as an index, maps, and historical commentary also needed to be included.
4. The protocol of having a chapter start on the right hand page would be dropped so that when the reader was holding the book they would see a picture(s) of the house and be able to read about it with a minimum of flipping pages.
5. The information needed to be correct. Facts needed to be checked, where they could not be confirmed that had to be noted to the readers and marked as lore or only having one source.

These families were often interconnected, which meant that there needed to be cross-referencing. The problem was how to cross reference to pages in books that have not even been started. The answer was easy – cross-reference based on the house. Therefore, when the reader sees (740 Br) it relates to the French family that lived in 740 Broadway. That system allows this book to reference families that will be written about in the future.

Selection as a Great Lady

Since readers would wonder why some houses were included while others, perhaps even bigger, were omitted, the criteria for a house to be integrated as one of the "Great Ladies" had to be consistent. The primary criteria were:

A. The building had to be currently standing – there are very few exceptions to this rule – only three in this book.

B. The building had to have been built as a house – the building could be an office, but it had to start out as a home.

C. Since the focus is on history rather than architecture, the houses should be built prior to 1920 – again, there would be a few exceptions.

D. The houses had to be visible from the sidewalk. The book would not encourage readers to go onto the current owners' property.

There were also reasons to exclude houses. Many current homes started out as carriage houses. The owners and architects are to be complimented on the transitions; however, because the original purpose of the buildings was not to be a family's home, they are excluded. There is some consideration for having a volume seven on the carriage houses.

While selecting the houses to be used as one of the "Great Ladies," it was apparent that some other, very interesting, smaller homes were nestled in to the neighborhoods. Although these houses may lack the grandeur of the bigger homes, they have a warm livable presence that reflects the period in which they were built. Because they are also a part of the city it was decided to include them as "debutants."

What's in a name?

Early in our country's history Saratoga was the name of the community that is now Schuylerville. To differentiate between the two hamlets and to build on the healthy waters, Saratoga Springs included the second word in its name. Since the people of the original Saratoga chose to change the community's name to honor Revolutionary War General Schuyler, there should be no confusion when Saratoga Springs is referred to in this series simply as Saratoga. To the readers who are purists, it is recognized that the official name is Saratoga Springs; however, to add the second word to a series of at least six books would add several pages and would provide no additional clarity.

Saratoga was incorporated as a city in 1915; prior to that it was a village. Since this book focuses on the period prior to 1920, in most cases Saratoga in this text will be referred to as a village.

Naming the houses

The naming of houses is interesting. Tour maps and some books on the history of Saratoga name the houses. The names chosen are unpredictable; sometimes they recognize the earliest owner, other times the most famous resident and there are times that the name is that of the family that owned the house the longest. Over the history of Skidmore College it owned several of the houses, especially the ones in the second volume. Skidmore tended to name the houses it owned after the family that donated it to the college.

Almost always the houses are now named after a family; however, in checking the old newspapers, many of the cottages had special names such as Tall Pines, Park Side or The Maples. In one of the later volumes the special names of the houses will be listed.

The name I chose for a house was based on the family that built the house; the one that lived in it the longest; one with an interesting story; or, if all else failed, the one living in it in 1895.

Why a particular story is told

Some of the houses in this series were summer cottages for the rich, while others belonged to local entrepreneurs and professionals. At the time these houses were built there was a sense of responsibility by those of the upper middle class to lead the community. For that reason the people who resided in the houses in this book were in essence the same people who fostered the city. Because they were actively involved in the city, they left a history that could be traced through newspaper accounts, where a day laborer would be much harder to learn about.

There will be readers who feel that the negative stories outweigh the positive. This is because the primary source was old newspapers; and newspapers rarely focus on good news.

Sources

The intention was to find a way for people to get to know Saratoga's neighbors, even though they have passed. To tell the story of a family that lived over a hundred years ago, there had to be a reliance on older books (some), newspapers (many), occasionally a scrapbook or picture. A list of the primary sources is included as a bibliography. If one is not mentioned it was inadvertent and will probably be picked up in one of the later books in the series. Keep in mind that this book was never written to be a textbook or research paper; therefore, it rarely has annoying footnotes. I have told my son that when I pass to find some willing recipient library or historian who would like my notes and give them to the public for future research. Be assured I did not make it up.

Saratoga was a late bloomer

Most cities the same age as Saratoga can trace their history to either a waterfall necessary to power mills, or proximity to the canals, rivers or a harbor for transportation. Being landlocked, in that it was not on an ocean, bay, river or lake, Saratoga did not start to grow as early as the other villages in the northeast. Even the distance from the village to the early canals retarded growth; however, the primary reason for the village's early growth can be attributed to water; mineral water.

Saratoga's growth and development, like all cities with a history dating back to the Revolution, was dependent on how people traveled especially to and from work. It is true that as cities grew there were trolleys and carriages but until the automobile, the primary method that village people used to get from place to place was walking. Since people were pedestrians, villages were concentrated. In Saratoga that meant that the early churches, stores, offices and hotels were built within a few blocks of one street, Broadway.

Although there were homes, taverns and boarding houses prior to 1800, Saratoga's most rapid growth followed the advent of mechanized travel; first, steamships brought guests up the Hudson River to Troy or Waterford where they could catch stages to the city. Later, visitors could travel by the railroads and the city's growth increased more rapidly. The impact of railroads to visitors is why so many houses in Saratoga are not colonial but rather were built thirty plus years after the Revolution.

Probably the best example of the relationship between growth and the economy of the city can be experienced by traveling east on Phila Street and continuing past were it becomes Fifth Avenue to where it ends on Henning Road. The first buildings were built prior to the civil war and on the last block they are still building as this book goes to press.

The size of the houses reflects the nation's and city's economy for the period in which they were built. There are virtually no houses on the streets that were built during the Great Depression and in the last decade owners have begun building grand homes and are even taking down homes to be replaced by bigger houses.

The early growth of Saratoga worked like a vice with Broadway as its shaft. The first taverns were built in the vicinity of what is at this writing the Old Bryan Inn. The site was chosen because it was near the High Rock Spring (the first discovered) and above the swampy area that is now a park. In the early 1800s other springs had been discovered in the area around Congress Park. Gideon Putnam, one of the principal men who helped make Saratoga a resort, took advantage of the newly discovered springs building his hotel at what is now Broadway and Washington Street. Early on the two sections were referred to as the "upper village" (north) and "lower village" (south). Over the next forty years the two areas grew together along Broadway. Once the intervening void was filled, Saratoga experienced early urban sprawl with the expansion out both ends of Broadway and to both the east and west.

Where many cities grew around their industries, the economy of Saratoga has always been particularly reliant on tourism; therefore, the village grew around its "industry" – the hotels. To maintain the attractiveness of Saratoga, industries, especially those that were noisy or dirty, were pushed to the outskirts. Although some of those early industrial sites are considered to be in the city today, they were at the fringes a hundred years ago.

Even in the late Victorian Age the renting houses in Saratoga during the season was common. Some of the people who owned the homes in this book and subsequent volumes could probably not have afforded to live in such grandeur had it not been for the summer income. During the Gilded Age and even beyond the *New York Times* and the *Saratogian* would have an article at the beginning of the season that was a list of who had rented each of the "cottages" in Saratoga.

How people lived has also changed

Housing and the size of properties have changed over the history of Saratoga. When Saratoga was still a small village, there were numerous townhouses built on Broadway and the early grand houses had small yards as demonstrated by the residences on Franklin Square. Prior to the Civil War there were some grand homes; however, they were nothing compared to the mansions that would follow in the 1870s through the outbreak of the First World War. As fortunes grew some of the more affluent of society wanted to demonstrate their wealth by being seen in carriages (the Mercedes or Cadillac of the day). To have a carriage, a house needed to have a second building for the horse. The small lots common in middle of the village would not accommodate a second structure so people started to build homes on larger lots that were on what was then the city's borders. This is demonstrated by the difference between the town homes included in this book that are on central

Broadway (the newest being 1878), as compared to the houses on North Broadway where construction of private homes started about the time it ended in the center of town.

This book is not about architecture but there was one common thread that, once noticed, is nearly impossible to miss. The earliest of homes were built without plumbing. When central heat became fashionable and with the modernization of plumbing, owners wanted to update the older homes. Some of the larger homes had pocket doors that could be opened for social occasions or closed in the winter to trap the heat but made the addition of pipes and electricity difficult. Many of the houses solved the problem by building an addition on the original house. This is probably most evident at 139 Circular (corner of Lake). The house is brick and the difference in the foundations and the seams in the brick clearly indicate the additions.

The missing block of history

Copies of the *Saratogian* from late 1890 through and including 1900 no longer exist. This loss has created a gaping hole in the documentation of Saratoga's history. Not only are the weddings, births and, more importantly to an historian, obituaries missing, so is the local perspective on the controversial issues of the period. Other newspapers in the area, principally those in Ballston Spa and Troy, covered the news from Saratoga but they can not give the community's perspective that would have been evident in the *Saratogian*.

What intensifies the loss is that the missing decade was a key period laden with issues that would confront and define Saratoga for the next fifty years. The missing decade was part of the temperance movement, an anti-gambling crusade, and an ongoing controversy over the future of the springs. Because of the moral nature of these issues, opinions on how they should be addressed created deep fissures between the residents of Saratoga. Newspapers from neighboring communities fill part of the gaps; however, the perspective is never the same as would have been given by a local newspaper.

Considering the accuracy of the lost history, one must remember that early issues of the *Saratogian* rarely carried what would be considered scandalous news. Saratoga, as a resort, needed to maintain its reputation for being a safe place. This is the reason that crimes, arrests and social miscues were rarely recorded in the early local newspapers.

History lost; history saved

Unfortunately, the homes of hotelier Gideon Putnam, merchant and postmaster Miles Beach, and Chancellor Reuben Walworth, whose visions of their city were so important to the early growth, are gone. Luckily, the homes of John Clarke, one of the earliest bottlers; the two Marvin brothers, bankers and owners of one of the hotels; and the home of George Batcheller, an international diplomat; are still standing for our generation to enjoy. The real test of our respect will be what an author a hundred years from today says about how we maintained the city these men left us.

Saratoga and water

Water was: the reason Saratoga Springs was late to grow; one of the primary reasons that it grew at all; in part responsible for the way it grew; and was almost the cause of its demise.

As old as the city may appear to visitors, in many ways Saratoga Springs is new city. By 1790, communities such as Albany, Schenectady, Troy and even smaller villages such as Ballston Spa, Schuylerville and Mechanicville were commercial centers while Saratoga was struggling to be considered a hamlet. Each of the other communities mentioned were on some body of water which could either be used for power or transportation. With only limited hills, and no major stream, Saratoga lacked waterfalls that could power the mills the way it had been harnessed in Ballston Spa, Mechanicville and Troy. Worse yet, the surface water Saratoga did have was largely a swamp that was in the valley beginning in the Congress Park and extending north along what is now Putnam and Henry Street out of town. Prior to the railroads the way goods were moved without being shaken up on pothole filled roads was over water; first on rivers (part of the reason for Albany and Schenectady) and later on canals (Schuylerville, Mechanicville and Whitehall).

Luckily, what resources Saratoga lacked in above ground water it made up for in underground water – the springs.

It was the mineral springs that were the principal attraction that started the city (coming for the waters was first – the social life of the hotels, racing and gambling followed). There is a section devoted to the growth of Saratoga, but even in the village, the model of industries being built near water was true. The difference was that the industry of Saratoga was the hotels which grew around not the flowing water but rather the springs.

Sylvester and the village directories indicate some of the history of the springs. In 1876 there were 25 springs in the city.

Although many tourists came to Saratoga to partake of the medicinal qualities of the springs, it was not the only way the waters were a resource to the community. John Clarke (46 Cr) opened the first soda fountain in the United States at 26 Wall Street in New York City. His formula was simple; he added flavors to carbonated water, selling what today is referred to as soda or pop. Realizing the value of the carbonated springs, Clarke moved to Saratoga taking over ownership of Congress Spring. He bottled and shipped water to other cities where it was sold both as spring water and as the base for soda.

As time progressed and railroad travel became popular, people with money escaped the heat of the cities by going to the country. Saratoga, because of its culture and the reputation it had for attracting some of the country's most important people, was literally one of the leading places in the nation to spend a part or all of the summer season. Among the visitors to the village were Presidents, Generals, Senators, Congressmen, industrialists and bankers. The American Bar Association was founded in Saratoga, along with a national bankers association.

Saratoga, which became a popular resort because of its water, almost lapsed into history because of a change in the use of water. At the beginning of the 1800s mineral water was believed to be medicinal. By the end of the century medications were coming into vogue and at the same time people were beginning to actually go swimming to relieve the heat of summer. In 1900, the resorts that were growing were places with beaches. Saratoga had no beaches and the old grand hotels did not have pools. The hard times the city experienced at the beginning of the 1900s were in part the result of the creation of a new article of clothing – the bathing suit.

Natural Gas – of another kind

In 1891 a spring owner developed a process that extracted the carbonation from the water. The carbon dioxide gas was then bottled and placed in large pressurized cylinders. The bottled carbon dioxide was shipped to cities where it was injected into water, beer and soda. The cost of shipping bottled gas was far below the cost of shipping carbonated water. Suddenly, some of the water that had built the village was a byproduct. Before the turn of the century there were four bottling plants that bottled not the water, but instead the gas.

This gas extraction process temporarily increased the value of the springs. The next step was logical; companies realized that they could save a step if they drilled down to the source of the springs and extracted the gas without ever taking the water out of the ground. It was an economic boom to the four companies that were involved.

Those who invested in the new gas extraction companies believed that the supply was unlimited. Not everyone in the village was thrilled with the concept of extracting the gas. In August of 1891, the *New York Times* interviewed the owner of the Empire Springs. He noted: "I am sorry. It will endanger the whole supply to let off so much of it (gas). If the springs run dry, good-bye to the property of Saratoga." The *Times* went on to say: "He is needlessly alarmed." The *Times* was wrong, the owner of the springs was right.

The problem was simple. The underground carbon dioxide was needed for pressure to force the water of all the springs to the surface. By 1900 the pressure on the springs was decreasing and there was a very serious concern about the long-term effect that drilling was having on the economy of the village. Everyone involved (except the gas companies) realized that there was a dangerous combination developing. It appeared that the decline in visitors started by the temporary ban on gambling in 1895 and the permanent ban of 1905, along with the aging hotels and the loss of the springs would not just hurt the tourist trade; it was a recipe that would finish the village.

As 1909 neared the springs almost went dry and Saratoga came close to experiencing the fate of the other spas in the state. The village would not just be reduced to a silhouette of its former grandeur, but confronted the possibility of becoming a ghost town. Luckily, the right people were living in the Saratoga and the village escaped the fate of its smaller counterparts (Richfield Springs and Sharon Springs).

There were several Saratogians involved in trying to stem the drilling for gas. Most notable among them on a national level was Spencer Trask, an investor and owner of Yaddo. The real person, however, who turned the tide was Charles Brackett (605 Br). At the time Brackett was an extremely influential State Senator, his power being in part gained by having been the campaign manager for then Governor Charles Evans Hughes. Brackett was able to push through a bill whereby the State would buy the land the gas bottlers stood on and create a reservation (referred to as the State Park) south of the village.

It was a bill that, at the time it passed, was divisive in the community. Those who owned or worked in the bottling plants opposed the bill, while those who owned the hotels felt it was the last hope. The number of tourists was already falling and many people with only limited financial interest in either the springs or the gas companies felt that the village was already doomed.

It is amazing the perspective one gains looking back at a decision made almost a century before. Over the next fifty years all the great hotels would be lost. The gas would surely have been long gone; thus the springs would have no longer percolated to the surface. The State Reservation, including the Gideon Putnam Hotel, golf course, car museum, museum of dance, and most of all SPAC, was a vision that did much to maintain what was to become the city.

Discovering and owning the springs

For those interested in greater detail there are numerous articles, papers and even sections of books about the qualities of the various springs in the region. The intention of this section is to provide a quick overview of how the springs impacted the village and its residents.

The reason that it took time to discover the various springs is that where they appeared on the surface was almost always in a swamp or at best a very damp area. In colonial times the entire valley that starts in Congress Park and proceeds northeast to the Northway was extremely marshy. It was in this boggy valley where most of the springs were located.

The name of the initial spring discovered, High Rock, literally explains why it was first; it bubbled out of a rock in the swamp, thus placing it above the marsh. The next two springs discovered were in the immediate vicinity of High Rock Spring. The discovery of these springs on the north end of the village and the desire of unhealthy visitors to be near the springs explains why the early growth of accommodations was in the upper village.

The Congress Spring was the first spring discovered further south. There is a legend as to who discovered this Congress Spring. Supposedly it was discovered in 1792 by Congressman Gilman from New Hampshire while out for a walk. During the 1800s Congress Spring was the most famous of the springs because of its taste and the perceived health benefits of the water. The discovery and resulting fame of the Congress Spring led to the building of three largest hotels in the lower village.

The springs that were eventually discovered in what is now the State Reservation came even later. By the time of the development of these springs, the hotels and Saratoga's social life were already established around Broadway. Since the new springs were out of the village, there was not a hotel building boom to the south of town like there had been in the upper and lower village.

As the swamp was slowly drained or foundations near the swamp were dug, new springs occasionally appeared. By 1876, **Sylvester** recognized twenty-five different springs in or near the village. They were: High Rock, Congress, Columbian, Empire, Excelsior, Union, Geyser (Spouting), Champion, Hathorn, Star, Vichy, Washington, Pavilion, Red, Hamilton, Saratoga "A", Kissingen, Eureka, Triton, United States, Triton, Magnetic, Seltzer,

Crystal, and Putnam. Since each had its own medicinal qualities it is easy to see why visitors were able to spend a week here and not drink from the same spring twice.

Several local fortunes were based on ownership of one or more of the springs. Ownership of a spring is treated like mineral rights. The spring belongs to the person who has title to the land on which it surfaces. Owning a spring was only beneficial if the proprietor had established some method of bottling and selling the water. The first operation was the tubing of the spring, a process that isolated the water and brought it to the surface through a pipe. It is the bottling and sale of the spring waters that explains why there was a plant in the village that manufactured glass bottles.

Since the springs had value the titles were exchanged over the years. Transfer of ownership explains why in the course of this series the names of several home owners will be associated with the same spring.

Renewable resources

Cities that experienced a boom because of a natural resource such as timber or the mining of some mineral learned that when that resource was consumed, they were to fall on hard times. Saratoga was fortunate, its natural resource was the springs, and they were renewable. It is to the natural resource of the numerous springs Saratoga can attribute much of its growth during its first century.

It was because of the benefits of the mineral waters that the hotels were built. Since one could hardly spend the entire day drinking water, Saratoga needed to develop ways to entertain its guests – a culture. The traditions that developed were built in two ways. There was the culture of the individual hotel and there was the culture of the village as a community. Each of the larger hotels had shops but there were also numerous privately owned stores lining Broadway and the surrounding side streets. The larger hotels would offer music and dances, but there was also a convention center, playhouse, orchestras and dancing. And for those less inclined toward the arts there was horse racing and the casinos.

Saratoga has been fortunate to attract another asset that historically kept renewing itself. That resource was the people who **chose** to reside within its borders. Like metal to a magnet, creative, wealthy and entrepreneurial people have consistently been drawn to Saratoga. Whether they came for the reputed health benefits, economic aspirations, the culture or professional associations, Saratoga, as a community, has for two centuries continually won the support of individuals who, because of their presence, have expanded the city's reputation. In reading this book it will become evident that most of those who built this city, and are doing so even today, made their fortunes somewhere else then moved to the city. The simple fact is Saratoga is an adopted city.

People have given Saratoga a national reputation – usually good

Over the years Saratoga has had among its residents: military leaders, state assemblymen, state senators, congressmen, senators, ambassadors and the widow of a former Vice President. There have even been those who were considered robber barons and those just considered robbers. To add to the mix, Saratoga's residents had influential friends. The Walworth's, Batchellers, Marvins, Bracketts, Beaches, Scribners and others could count among their friends Presidents, Supreme Court Justices, governors, authors, industrialists, bankers, entrepreneurs, film makers and social leaders. The interpersonal relationships of the people living in Saratoga brought other people to the city and have thus given Saratoga national influence.

One of the village's residents, Major Leland, proprietor of the Grand Union Hotel, was General Grant's aid de camp. Another summer resident, Joseph Drexel, provided President Grant with a cottage to finish his memoirs. For years after Grant's death, veterans who felt that his leadership had saved the Northern cause came to Saratoga and to Mt. McGregor as part of tribute to their fallen hero.

On the other end of the political spectrum are survivors of Tammany Hall. After Boss Tweed was removed, Edward Kearney (156 Caroline) was one of the leaders of New York City's Democratic Party. Looking at his home one appreciates how far a butcher can climb. Orphaned at a young age, John McBride Davidson, built his fine Victorian Mansion (203 Union), from the proceeds of his business building safes – after he gave Tweed's daughter a $5,000 bracelet for a wedding present he received a contract to provide safes for buildings owned by the City of New York.

It is only natural that a city that ignored gambling, hosted Presidents, and healed or at least reduced the symptoms of hundreds should have an interesting status.

Why 1895?

Life and societies change. In writing a book about the families that lived in a city, it is difficult to fully grasp their accomplishments appropriately in the context of the history or economy of their community unless there is a reference point [e. g. the discovery of a spring in 1809 was much more significant than discovering one in 1890]. In all communities there are milestone years; these landmarks are usually economic such as the opening or closing of a mill or business. 1895 was such a year for Saratoga; it was the year the city first tried seriously to eliminate gambling. It was the wrong decision at the wrong time.

Background - In the early 1890s the nation was entering a period of social reform with organized groups seeking to change morality through social legislation. The first two institutions attacked were gambling and the consumption of alcohol. New York State even went so far as to pass a law prohibiting barbershops from opening on Sundays, thinking that would push men to attend church services. It was not that gambling was legal; the problem was that individual communities, like Saratoga, were not enforcing the State's ban. The casinos were so accepted that Saratoga was often referred to as the Monte Carlo of America. *Gambling on horse racing was usually a separate debate from games of chance.*

Those supporting reforms were sure that gambling was a menace to the community and that a ban would have no affect on the tourist trade. The reformers were convinced that each person turned off by the loss of gambling would be replaced by someone else who wanted a family oriented environment.

Change - In 1895 a slate of reform candidates was elected in the city. As soon as they took office, the new trustees assured those who owned and operated the casinos that the State's law against gambling would be rigorously enforced. One by one the owners, including Canfield, announced that they would not open for the summer. For the first time the major casinos were closed. There was a debate among the village trustees to restrict horse racing but it failed.

Several of the lake houses on Saratoga Lake had a history of gambling. These lake houses were out of the jurisdiction of the village trustees but they were also out of town and not convenient.

Economics - During the Victorian Era there were no credit cards and people were more reluctant to go into personal debt, so resorts were dependent of the national economy. When the anti-gambling candidates were elected Saratoga was only beginning to recover from the depression of 1893.

Americans have always been attracted to new, more modern facilities and social activities. By 1895, Congress Hall and the United States Hotel were both thirty years old. Even the renovations of the Grand Union were twenty years old. Families that had always come to Saratoga for the season found that they were being attracted to other, more modern resorts. Although older people were still interested in the affects of the mineral springs, younger people were after newer uses for water, such as sailing, sculling and swimming. Ocean resorts such as Long Beach, Newport, Atlantic City, the Hamptons and even Cape May offered the breezes of the ocean, swimming and modern accommodations. These resorts were growing while the interest in Saratoga was waning.

The elimination of gambling pulled down the reservations at the hotels. People, especially the men, sought out resorts with more options. Without single men, single women were less interested in the city. Attendance at the track was so low that the last dates of the season were almost cancelled. While the other resorts boomed, Saratoga struggled for the season.

The next year the voters removed the reform candidates. Unfortunately, the decision to end gambling, for even the one year, would place the city on a downward slide that would continue for decades.

A day in the Spa City

Saratoga's first hay-day was a time when there were no televisions, I-pods, electronic games and the hotels did not even have pools. People, especially kids, get bored even when they are surrounded by today's electronic distractions. Among their calls of "I'm bored," it is only natural to wonder what it was like in 1894 (note year) for the 40,000 people who might be spending a day in Saratoga. There is no simple answer because the way visitors occupied their time changed based on the person's age, gender and the decade they were in the village. There are, however, some generalizations.

Until two hundred years ago virtually everyone in the United States lived on a farm with daily chores; therefore, the concept of a vacation is a relatively new social phenomenon. The first people to "get away" often did so for their health, which is why the earliest visitors came to "take the waters." The first guests either had maladies of their own or they were accompanying someone who did. In either case the person was here primarily for the healing effects of the springs. One can only drink so much water, but since health was the universal purpose for every visitor in the village and because the first hotels were relatively small, people actually met on the porches and lobbies and talked to the other guests. If the person's health was up to it, they might take a walk or ride out into the countryside or to the lake.

Saratoga and the other spas offered something not available in the small communities that were home to most Americans. The spas were a place where someone could easily meet, walk and talk with new acquaintances. With a trip to the spas one's child was exposed to people (politely said potential partners) from other communities. It was not long before Saratoga had a reputation as a place to find suitable partners. The other advantage Saratoga offered was the natural screening made by the prices of various the hotels. Staying in an expensive hotel improved the possibility that the person your child met was financially solid. Such natural selection did no insured that there were interlopers who were trying to improve their lot. Part of the mating game played at the balls and social events of each season became screening; those who were appropriate from those who were unsuitable.

As more people started coming to Saratoga, there was an increased need for entertainment. Eventually, a daily routine or culture developed. By the time Saratoga was 50 years old it was already the place to see and be seen. Therefore many of the activities of each day were designed around being out among the throng.

Each morning before breakfast, the village's guests would take a morning stroll where they would either go to one of the springs or to the Hall of Springs to "take the water."

At 8:00 breakfast was served – banquet style. In the beginning everyone in the hotel was served at the same time.

After the morning meal people would gather on the piazzas or in the courtyards of the hotels where they wrote letters, read the newspaper or a book. As the village grew there was shopping to be done at the numerous stores in town.

Lunch was served at 1:00 – again banquet style.

In the afternoon there would often be a musician performing in the courtyard of the hotel; people could rent carriages and go to the lake, and after the Civil War there was horse racing for the men. Since horse racing involved gambling and women and children were discouraged from attending, the village started putting on tennis tournaments and an annual regatta. In the social structure of the day there were often teas and other events women guest in the afternoon.

In both the afternoon and the morning there were a series of bath houses open. These establishments offered Turkish and Russian Baths among others.

In 1905 the number of cars in Saratoga quadrupled over the year before; the number went from 60 to 250. For the men it was the rage to rent a car and take the girl they admired for a ride around town or out to the lake. For those who think traffic on Broadway is bad now, imagine what it was like when there were hundreds of wagons and carriages and 250 cars, 200 of which were rented by people who had never driven a car before.

Dinner was served at 6:00 – again banquet style.

After dinner there was activity that, although not quite mandatory, was generally practiced. It was the evening stroll up and down Broadway. The walkways in front of the hotels were often so crowded that one took the first opportunity to squeeze in and moved at the same pace as the crowd.

Later in the evenings there were hops, performances by the hotels' orchestras, and plays. For the men there was the casino that is now a museum in the park and other gambling places, the locations of which have been lost.

At the better hotels women changed for each meal, the evening event, and if there was a tea or social in the afternoon they would again change. This meant that women had to have three to five changes of clothes each day. There was a the story of a woman who had to check out of her hotel after one week because she only brought 45 dresses and it was her practice never to wear the same outfit on the porch of her hotel twice. There is no record of how much her spouse gambled.

The city is unique

Much of the elegance of the Saratoga can be credited to some of the earlier inhabitants. The development of Congress Park and the tree lined streets were in part the efforts of John Clarke, who drained the swamp that is now Congress Park to bottle and market the waters of his spring. Dr. Clarke pushed a law giving a tax break for people who planted trees along the street in front of their homes. The Clarke house, at 46 Circular Street, stands proudly as a testament to its owner's vision. The casino and race track, which are enjoyed by locals and visitors alike, were primarily the creation and vision of John Morrissey and John Canfield. State Senator Edger Brackett (605 Br) realized the importance of the mineral waters to the city. Brackett used his considerable influence to convince the State to build the State Reservations south of town. Lucy Scribner envisioned a liberal arts college for women (Skidmore). Saratoga owes much to these peoples' combined vision (note none of these people were born in Saratoga).

It was, however, its citizens who ultimately made Saratoga Springs thrive while other resorts built around their springs (Richfield Springs, and Sharon Springs) passed from grandeur with the short-lived "taking of the waters." Saratoga has succeeded because it has consistently been able to attract the type of people who build, not just sustain, a community. The affect of new residents is evident by those who lived in the early houses that are now lost to Broadway. At one time, some of the leading lawyers in the nation lived within a few blocks of each other on or near Broadway. As an example within a block on Broadway there was Walworth, the last Chancellor of the courts of New York who was nominated for the Supreme Court (he was not appointed) lived where the property has been converted to a gas station. William A. Beach, one of Vanderbilt's lawyers and major criminal lawyer in the Victorian Era, lived in a house on the property now occupied by the Post Office. Esek Cowen lived a block off Broadway.

Accommodations

In 1895, the New York Times stated that Saratoga had lodging for 40,000 guests. The same year there were only 9 restaurants listed in the village directory.

There are numerous pictures of the United States Hotel, Congress Hall, and the Grand Union. Clearly, these were the three principal hotels and the ones most associated with the city. Over the course of Saratoga's history, however, there were many more places to stay. According to the Directory of Saratoga Springs, in 1895 there were 48 hotels within the village with two more on the lake. The same year there were over 80 named boarding houses. Additionally, there were other options besides the places that advertised that they would accept guests. After the Civil War, homes of all sizes were available to rent. In the Victorian Era, those who owned property in the village found that during the "season" they were very popular with friends and family looking for a place to enjoy the culture. People who live here today realize that things have not changed very much.

Hotels – Boarding Houses - Homes

The first public accommodations were in the vicinity of High Rock Spring at the corner of Rock and Putnam Street (Old Bryan Inn). The discovery of Congress Spring resulted in a second set of hotels being built in the vicinity of what is now Congress Park.

Until Putnam started building his hotel in 1809, there were only accommodations for at most a couple of hundred people in the entire village. By the 1890s the United States Hotel had 768 rooms and 65 suites; the Grand Union could house 2,000 guests; Congress Hall claimed to have 600 rooms capable of holding 1000 guest at $3 - $4 a night for room and board. Their little sister, The Adelphi, had accommodations for 150 guests with rooms costing between three and five dollars a day. The Adelphi advertised that it had new plumbing, hot and cold running water and free transportation to and from the railroad station. By contrast the fifty rooms at The Circular Street House (103 Cr) rented for $8 to $12 a week including board.

Dr. Strong's Sanitarium, which was a medical institute on the corner of Circular and Spring Streets could host 200 guests at a cost $2.50 to $3.50 per day or $14 to $21 a week. In addition to the clean air, the sanitarium provided a sun parlor, roof garden, Turkish and

Russian Baths, lawn tennis, croquet, billiards and a gym.

In addition to boarding houses, some middle class widows were able to maintain their homes by renting rooms to "select guests" in the summer. Visitors enjoyed these private homes because the service was personal; the quality accommodations; and the quietness of the rooms compared to those at the hotels.

Saratoga's hotels worked on the American Plan so the cost of meals was included in the daily rate. Since the meals were all served in the hotel, guests from the different hotels would compare the menus and discuss the preparation and service. There was competition for the best chefs as families would change hotels to have better meals or service.

In the best hotels each family had an assigned table. In other hotels seating was on a first come first served basis. Open seating allowed for more opportunities to meet new people, but also meant that one could not be assured of the manners of the others at the table.

Until the 1870s, in all the hotels every guest was served at the same time. Toward the end of the century the practice of everyone in the hotel eating at the same time started breaking down. The United States was the first hotel to extend the times initiating two hour serving blocks; breakfast was from 7:00 until 9:00; lunch from noon until two o'clock; and dinner from six o'clock until eight. By the end of the century many of the hotels' dining rooms were open from seven in the morning until midnight.

The hotel was not just a place to sleep, it was a social center. The larger hotels each had an orchestra and musicians that would play during the day. The larger hotels had their own stores, could arrange a carriage for an outing, and would provide other services.

Most of the hotels and virtually all the boarding houses were operated by the owner. For the first fifty years the United States Hotel was family owned and operated by the Marvin family. During the same period, both the Congress Hall and Grand Union had several owners. The arrangements necessary in booking musicians, assigning guests to their rooms and generally operating a hotel which served thousands of meals a day was stressful. Over time some of the hotels hired professional managers or would lease out the operations of the hotel in a contractual arrangement where by the owners received a fixed amount for the season or took some part of the profits.

The proprietor of a hotel was not just a manager; he was sometimes a social arbitrator making the position powerful but thankless. At a time when a hotel such as the main three in the village housed a thousand guests, the assignment of rooms became a true nightmare. The wealthy and the wealthy want-to-be's expected the same rooms year after year, even if they came for a different period. One year an extended family might all get along and want adjacent rooms. The next year there might have been a family dispute and the hotel was expected to move one part of the family to different quarters; and no family member wanted to be the one to move. To make it worse, every one who could afford it wanted the room down the hall from Commodore Vanderbilt.

The problem for the hotels in Saratoga was keeping pace with the public's "rapid" changes in expectations. The first change, which seems archaic today, was to install the plumbing required for gas lighting. Later the hotels were expected to have elevators, electric lights, individual bathrooms – not just a common one down the hall. In the grand hotels these changes required retrofitting; in the smaller hotels some of these expectations were nearly impossible. Over time, Saratoga's grand hotels aged and although they still possessed much of the dignity for which they were famous, their glitter was disappearing and eventually they lost the competition to the newer hotels in the newer resorts.

By the 1870s the very wealthy were getting tired of eating with everyone else in the hotel; listening to the noises both in the hotel and on the street; and getting an unfamiliar carriage from the livery. Some families bought or built cottages that were only opened during the season; the problem was they were vulnerable to weather and theft in the off season. A new practice of renting private houses resolved both problems. Renting one's home offered both parties an interesting option. Now residents could rent their houses for the six to ten weeks of the season and receive enough to stay somewhere else and still maintain the houses the rest of the year for no cost. Those who rented the houses had to arrange for their own meals and entertainment, but out of the hotel they were in a better position to manage their own family and affairs. Many of the very wealthy brought their own staff with them when they rented a cottage in Saratoga, which meant they wanted the largest available house. Since the houses of the professionals and merchants were the largest and best suited to those of money, they were the first to rent. The problem for the Saratogians who were in commercial enterprises was that the season was when they most needed to be near their businesses.

There were common options practiced by Saratogians who rented out their homes. Some families traveled or descended on family out of the area. Other families went to camps on lakes in the Adirondacks. A few actually rented their home for enough to stay in one of less expensive hotels in the village. Many, maybe even most, had summer camps out on Saratoga lake.

What the ability to rent out one's house did was allow the merchants and professionals in the village to live in better homes than they would have been able to had they not had the additional income.

In 1895 during the year, the trains from New York City to Saratoga took almost exactly five hours. The Saratoga Limited, an express, ran three times a day during the "season" with runs that took three and a half hours.

Connections

One of the most commonly asked question is why did people start coming to Saratoga? The answer is obviously the waters and clean air. The secondary question is what about those who were not here for the waters? That answer is more subtle. In large part they came because of the connections that the village afforded. Those connections could be social, political, economic or even cultural but, since the first hotels, there has always been a strong and important interpersonal aspect to Saratoga.

Forming connections probably started more by coincidence than design. Some of the early guests were too ill or unwilling to travel alone, so they came to Saratoga accompanied by a younger, healthier family member. As those who were ill rested, their healthier assistants would gather on the porches and in the lobbies of the hotels. These people all had one thing in common; they were caring for someone else. Their common mission created a bond which made starting a conversation with a stranger acceptable. It was not long until accompanying an ill person who to Saratoga was recognized as an opportunity to meet someone to marry; or with whom to start a business; or just form a friendship.

Before 1870, Saratoga was already acknowledged as one of the premier social centers during the season. The Spa's reputation attracted people from throughout the country. In the resorts, and especially Saratoga, it was anticipated that people, both men and women, were visiting with the intention of taking part in the social and cultural functions. Starting with everyone eating at the same time continuing to the weekly dance, the activities in each of the hotels were set up to facilitate being seen. During the Victorian Era the popular dances were arranged so that during the course of a single composition men and women had a variety of partners.

Saratoga, during the Victorian Era, could legitimately be considered a marrying zone. It was less acknowledged but better understood that resorts were a place to bring your children (especially a daughter) to meet eligible suitors. Because America was primarily rural, in a family's home community there were a limited number of available people from which to choose a partner. Since Saratoga was a place where you were supposed to be seen and meet people, it was only natural that families would come here the year their children were of a marrying age.

The varying costs of the hotels in Saratoga served as a natural screening devise. It was reasonable to assume that someone staying for the whole season in the United States or the Grand Union was far more suitable than a person staying for a week at one of the less exclusive addresses. To keep score of the relationships that were formed there were a group of dowagers sat on the porches of the hotels for the entire summer.

The professions, especially the law, also brought people to Saratoga. Before law colleges, aspiring attorneys studied under men in the profession. The practice was called "reading for the bar." Among Saratoga's residents were several well recognized attorneys. Included in the group of esteemed attorneys were Judge William Warren, Judge Esek Cowen, and Chancellor Rueben Walworth; later names included William A. Beach and Augustus Bockes. To read under any of these men was a virtual assurance of appointment to the bar and a successful career. These men brought to the community leadership in one of the professions and leagues of followers.

New York State's highest court, the Court of Appeals, held its spring session in Saratoga. The judges would stay at the Walden Hotel. Lawyers that were arguing cases would stay at various hotels throughout the village. Lawyers appearing before the court, who may not have visited the village before, were exposed to all the opportunities that the Spa afforded.

Although people studied medicine in much the same way as they read for the bar, Saratoga did not enjoy the same reputation among the physicians who were residents. This is surprising since it would be expected that the perceived medicinal properties of the springs would attract a group of doctors who would have been widely acclaimed.

It was, however, in economic and political opportunities that the inspirations of Saratoga truly shone. Each season there were Presidents or those who aspired to the office, Senators, Congressmen, Ambassadors and Governors visiting the city to either shore up support or try to gain endorsement for future offices. Members of New York City's infamous Tammany Hall came each year to the Spa treating like their private club.

Those who dreamed of economic opportunity were drawn to Saratoga like metal to a magnet because of the combination of the impact of individuals like railroad tycoons Commodore Vanderbilt and Jay Gould, banker Joseph Drexel or August Belmont; each of whom visited every summer.

To understand how influential Saratoga was as a place to be seen, one only needs to see who visited the city in the summer of 1865. In late July, General Grant, who had accepted Lee's surrender only three months before, visited the village. Grant's arrangements in the city demonstrated that he was a natural politician. He stayed at the Congress Hotel, but ate his meals at the Grand Union, the United States had burned months before. At the Grand Union, Grant was the guest of Major Leland (the proprietor), who had been one of his staff officers during the war. James Marvin proprietor of the United States Hotel presented the General with a box of cigars. Also in Saratoga at the same time were Generals Winfield Scott, Carr, and Jerome. In the village that summer, there was a dinner to honor Grant. Included among those who attended were such notables as Cornelius Vanderbilt and Thurlow Weed.

The opinions in this section are those of the author. Others might claim a different sequence of reasons for visiting. It is an open debate, one I would enjoy engaging in.

The Civil War
Was local

Many of the men who lived in the houses that comprise Saratoga's Great Ladies served in the War of the Rebellion (its name during and for several years after the conflict). If not, they almost always had immediate family who had been in the military service. There is a background point about civil war service that needs to be understood. Despite the fact that most of the battles were fought south of the Mason Dixon Line, the war had a very local element unlike service today. That component was that people from communities served together.

When Lincoln sent out his call for volunteers to form what would be called the Army of the Patomac, communities throughout the north raised their own companies. Four companies in the 77th New York were raised in Saratoga. These companies were men who had grown up together and for good or ill, their families knew each other.

There were two dramatic effects of localized enlistment and service. During the war, if a particular company had severe losses in a given engagement, that meant that their home community shared at the same level; there were communities both north and south where a major portion of the young men were lost in a given battle. There was a second more long term effect. Since, after the war, the soldiers often returned to their native communities everyone in the area knew the degree of each man's valor or lack thereof. Twice Colonel French (740 Br) suffered minor wounds but he never left the field during a battle; a record that would be noted and remembered. The entire community grieved when young Captain Luther Wheeler was killed valiantly on the field. The letter Colonel French wrote, which appeared in the *Saratogian*, explaining that he had tears in his own eyes at the loss of Wheeler. This admission was never interpreted as a weakness but rather a tribute to a fallen hero.

A third effect was on the people left behind. Since many of the men were serving together, there were campaigns to raise money for blankets, bandages, or other necessities. These were assured of reaching those for whom they were intended.

The real long term effect of the Civil War was the Grand Army of the Republic (GAR), a predecessor of the American Legion. This was a nationwide brotherhood of veterans that formed after the war and met regularly in most northern communities. Membership in the GAR was limited to men who had served in the Civil War. The GAR was politically active supporting candidates for offices from local mayors up to the President. So deep was the association between the men who had served that the GAR was a social and political force for forty years. In most communities, and even Saratoga, the endorsement of the GAR was essential for election to public office. Saratoga's GAR was named in honor of Captain Luther Wheeler (630 Br).

The 77th

The companies from each state were traditionally numbered in sequence. Thus the third New York volunteered long before the 183rd. Saratoga's volunteer company, the 77th New York, was unique in one respect. The number 77 was assigned in honor of the Battle of Saratoga which took place in 1777; if numbered in sequence Saratoga's regiment would have been in the 40s.

Over 250 men from Saratoga Springs and surrounding towns enlisted into the 77th New York. The company's losses were so great that at one point during the war while Col. French was home of leave to recover his personal health, one of his official responsibilities was to recruit new men to replace those who had been killed, wounded, or sent home for illness. The 77th New York is always associated with Saratoga; however, a look at the record shows that nearly as many local men served in the 30th New York.

Other local citizens served in other companies, the cavalry, artillery, and navy.

Gambling in the Spa

Without a doubt one of the most commonly asked questions is: "When did gambling become illegal in Saratoga?" The answer is at the same time it became illegal everywhere else in New York State, 1851. What the inquirer is usually seeking to know, however, is when did the Saratoga police start enforcing the State's gambling laws? – That has a very different answer.

Although a community can pass a law that is more restrictive than its state, it can not pass a local ordinance that is in violation of a state statute. For that reason Saratoga should have started enforcing the State's anti-gambling laws as soon as they were passed.

What happened in Saratoga was that the laws were only occasionally enforced. In Saratoga the State laws that restricted gambling were ignored except when there was a complaint about a game being unfair. There are cases in the 1880s where gambling houses in Saratoga were raided in the height of the season and the equipment confiscated because patrons felt they were cheated or duped. At the same time Canfield's "club," which was known for having fair games, ran without interference.

The exception was every few years, if there was a political challenge for the office of district attorney. Then the incumbent would be sure that there were arrests for gambling in the September or October preceding the election.

The social tolerance was because most people considered gambling to be a wink crime; everyone knew it was going on but since it was considered as victimless, people acknowledged it with a wink. Drunkenness and prostitution are other crimes that at the same time were usually treated as wink crimes; people knew they happen but the laws were basically ignored.

Types of gambling

Gambling appears in many different forms and in Saratoga it took on almost all of them. From sports betting to cards; from the horses to the casinos; in the 1880s a person who did not live in the village could bet on almost anything. The key concept is that the person betting was not supposed be from Saratoga. Like all communities, Saratoga was concerned about its residents having problems as a result of losing at games of chance. To avoid a problem within the community the more upscale gambling halls, like Canfield's, required those who wanted to get inside show their room key. *My great-grandfather and his brother, who both lived less than ten miles outside the village, twice each summer would take a room at one of the hotels just so they could have a key to get into the casinos; based on their respective homes neither won very much money.* Once inside the casinos there were none of the brilliantly colored video games; instead, people had to settle for card tables, faro wheel, roulette, or played dice. One of the most common forms of sports betting was boxing, although patrons could bet on baseball and other sports.

Since people did not carry large sums of cash, gambling in Saratoga was based on mutual trust. The gamblers had to believe the games were fair and the club owners had to believe the gamblers would pay any markers they might incur. There were stories of people betting and losing vast amounts of money at Canfield's; however, it was hard to file a complaint against the establishment since the loser would have to admit that he (women were not permitted to bet) had entered a building knowing it was in violation of the law. On the other hand it was hard for Canfield or any of the other owners to legally enforce a debt, since they would have to admit that it was incurred at an illegal activity.

Gambling was such an accepted activity that in 1894 the president of the village (mayor today) openly operated a local "resort."

In 1895 a group of reformed-minded citizens pushed a slate of candidates who advocated that the State's anti-gambling laws be enforced. The reformers won and for one year the gambling halls were all closed. The next year the reformers were all removed from office (see Why 1895).

With the reformers out of office, gambling resumed in varying degrees until 1905. That year the issue moved up a level in government when the Governor insisted that the anti-gambling laws be upheld. What the local community might tolerate was not acceptable to the higher level of government. The casinos in the city, which were easy to observe, closed. The action moved out to the more isolated lake houses for the next two decades.

G. F. Harvey Company
A little thing that makes so much money

George F. Harvey, a native Vermonter, worked in the Midwest following the Civil War as a pharmaceutical salesman. In that capacity he came to understand that rural doctors and apothecaries had a consistent set of problems with their prescription medicines. He would make his fortune solving that set of problems.

There were three different issues that confronted those responsible for medications; dosage, keeping the various medicines separated, and shelf life. The problems of dosage and shelf life were exacerbated in rural areas where there were fewer patients. Since medicines in the Victorian Era came either as a liquid or powder, there was no way of ensuring that a patient took the appropriate dosage (not all families, especially those who were poor, had measuring spoons). Storage was a problem since the various elements in air, including oxygen, reacted fairly quickly with exposed fine particles of the powders. Adding to the problem were the horror stories about pharmacies mixing up the medications. Drugs were usually stored alphabetically and often there were errors because other drugs stored nearby were spelled similarly. *A wealthy female patient of Dr. Strong (88 Cr) died as a result of his providing the medicine that was alphabetically next to the one he wanted.*

The answer was something taken for granted today-
the common pill.

In the early 1880s George F. Harvey who had relocated to Saratoga was living in a house on Church Street. At approximately the same time he met a man who had developed a process that took prescription powders and converted them into pill form. Realizing the need for pre-measured medicines Harvey bought the rights and started producing pills in his kitchen out of what, at the time, were common powdered remedies such as aspirin. He would then take his new pills in his carriage traveling to stores and doctors in the area and sell them already bottled. Harvey's product created what was literally an eureka moment. Suddenly pharmacists did not need to measure out prescription medicines, shelf life improved and there was far less likelihood of a patient taking the wrong dosage. Harvey was one of those stories of a person who began working out of his kitchen and wound up a millionaire.

Soon Harvey's product line (the number of medications available in pill form) was growing and his distribution network was expanding (the area in which he was selling his product). He found that by using positive, aggressive salespeople he was able to have his products appear on the shelves of most rural stores. It was not long before the demand for Harvey's pills exceeded his individual ability to produce them or his financial ability to expand his operation. The natural answer was to incorporate. The resulting business, G. F. Harvey Company, was financed by local investors who, although often comfortable before they invested, over the next decade would become wealthy. Some of the investors include; Edgar Brackett (605 Br); Sidney Richard (634 Br); James Mingay (491 Br & 100 Lake); and William Bockes (34 Cr). There were other Saratogians who were smaller investors.

G. F. Harvey Co.'s main operation in Saratoga was located at 7 Wells Street. At that site the company had a lab, production facilities and its central headquarters. As the decade of the 1890s progressed the company continually expanded. Soon G. F. Harvey Company was setting up regional operations in Canada, the Midwest and eventually the West coast.

G. F. Harvey left the business before 1900 starting the National Pill Company that would be located in Philadelphia. He took with him a fortune and left behind a business that would thrive for another seventy years.

BROADWAY

563

Hewitt

Built as the home and office of physician Adelbert Hewitt this house has had an interesting cycle going from a high as the residence of a professional person to offices supporting a social services program. It is now enjoying a rebirth.

Hewitt, like many of his neighbors, was interested in the future of Saratoga. Although not on the slate himself, Hewitt was one of the men who supported the reforms of 1895, which attempted to end gambling in the village. The reformers were voted out the next election.

In 1904-05, Hewitt was a member of an unofficial group referred to as the Committee of Fifteen. The committee was comprised of some of the leading citizens in the village who challenged two men who were commissioners on the Street, Water and Sewer Commission. The allegations held that the two commissioners had exceeded their power and misused city workers. The charges were finally aired in 1905 with one commissioner, Annis, virtually exonerated and the other embarrassed (Moriarta).

Annis was not one to have his name appear in the newspaper and not rebel. When the village trustees failed to support the allegations against him, he sued the members of the Committee of Fifteen for libel. Annis received little more than a public apology for his efforts but he had made those who had challenged him see what it felt like to have their names in the newspaper. As Annis' case was ending Hewitt left Saratoga and moved to Fort Edward.

The house later became the Salvation Army. It has recently been revamped by a local builder who has restored it to its former grace.

BROADWAY

569

Ames

George L. Ames was a man who found success in three totally different professions. Born in Becket, Massachusetts, Ames attended Black River Academy in Vermont before moving to Schuylerville where he opened a jewelry store (1852). His store was successful enough that he was able to support himself and his wife while he was simultaneously reading for the law and serving as town clerk.

In 1857, while operating his jewelry business and studying for the bar, he was appointed commissioner of the Champlain Canal; one of the shortest in the state. He would later give up that position to be the deputy commissioner of the eastern branch of the Erie Canal. An inventor, he developed several improvements for the locks on the canals.

He was admitted to the bar in 1861 immediately selling his store. In 1870 he came to Saratoga where he worked as a lawyer. On at least three occasions he was appointed receiver when businesses went bankrupt. He was the receiver for the Commercial Bank of Saratoga (1875), also for the American Hotel and the Geyser Spring. He was also the president of the Schuylerville National Bank. One of his more unusual appointments was in being selected to lay out the grounds for the Prospect Hill Cemetery in Schuylerville and Greenridge Cemetery in Saratoga.

George died in 1894 and his widow Helen, called Ellen, lived until 1932; she was 97. The couple had no children but have one of the largest plots in Greenridge Cemetery.

BROADWAY

577

Baucus

The man who lived in this house was, Joseph Baucus who made his living as a potato dealer and as a very successful farmer in Bacon Hill. Active in politics, Joseph served as Justice of the Peace (1849); a county supervisor for ten terms including having been selected as moderator in 1861; at one time he was also the Sheriff. After his first wife died Joseph's son, Alexander, took over the family farm. At approximately the same time Joseph remarried and moved to Saratoga. Joseph died in 1885 and his widow, Mary, lived in this house for over half a century.

In addition to his farm, Joseph's son, Alexander, was a potato dealer. He would buy potatoes from the farmers in Washington County and ship them to New York City. Baucus was a State Assemblyman, and twice was elected county Sheriff. Alexander would serve as State Senator from 1882-83. When Alexander, a Democrat, learned the Republicans were planning to run a candidate against him, he refused to stand for re-election and his political career was over. Alexander was a significant witness in the trial of Jesse Billings (To Spend Eternity Alone).

It is, however, Joseph Baucus' grandson, Joseph D., who leaves us the most anguishing tale. Born in 1865, Joseph D. sought to become a lawyer. He moved in with his step-grandmother in Saratoga so he could read for the law in one of the local law offices. In February of 1890 at the age of 25, Joseph D. married Emma Olney of Rome, New York. The Olneys were one of the wealthier families in Rome. In the fashion of the day the young couple went on a honeymoon trip; however, this trip was unusual. They escorted the bride's mother to Chicago where she boarded a train bound for her son's home in Colorado. With mom gone the newlyweds boarded the Lake Shore Limited and started for their new home in Saratoga.

On the return trip the conductors noticed that the cars were behaving erratically and surmised that some of the passenger cars had been uncoupled from the main train. In the front section, the conductor pulled the cord which signaled the engineer to stop the train, which he did.

There was a second conductor in the back section who also realized that the train had uncoupled. He tried to pull the airbrakes to no avail. He ran to the hand brake reaching it exactly as the two sections collided. The back cars of the train smashed into the front cars of the same train. The scene that followed was traumatic to all who witnessed it.

Joseph and Emma were seated together in one of the coaches when the two sections collided. Joseph's face and leg were badly bruised; however, Emma had been literally crushed by the impact. When medical help arrived Joseph begged them to save his wife. The physicians could tell by the extent of the injuries that there was nothing they could do for Emma, so they laid her across several of the seats making her last moments as comfortable as possible. As others stood by Joseph kept kissing the bloody face of his bride. Emma, along with seven others, died at the scene.

Two days later Emma was laid out in the living room of her parents' home. It was the same room where she had been married less than a week before. It was said that virtually everyone at the funeral could not help but weep.

Joseph would return to his step-grandmother's house for a couple of years but he would never remarry.

About 1893, Joseph moved his practice to New York City joining a law firm on Wall Street. He, along with a partner, Frank MaQuire, formed the Continental Commerce Company. For a brief time in 1894, it appeared that Joseph would make his own fortune when his company gained the international rights to Edison's Kinetoscope (an early form of movie projector). Unfortunately, Edison had failed to patent his machine outside of North America and the machine was copied around the word.

Mrs. Baucus would stay in the house well past 1910. To defer the cost she would take in women as boarders.

BROADWAY

581

Freeborn

Built in 1834, this is believed to be one of the oldest houses in Saratoga. Its longevity may be due in part to the fact that during the building's first 100 years it belonged to three generations of the same family.

Samuel Freeborn, the first generation, was a stone mason. During the period Freeburn lived in this house Saratoga experienced a construction boom in the commercial sector. Masons were in demand to set the foundations for multi-story hotels, numerous commercial buildings and later the grand cottages. Even after the hotels were constructed masons were busy helping them to stay competitive by constantly putting on additions, palazzos, and placing walkways for their grounds.

The early hotels and commercial businesses were wood framed buildings whose life expectancy was frequently shortened by fire. That was the case when both the United States burned in 1865 and Congress Hall burned in 1866. In the case of the Congress Hall the fire was the night before it was scheduled to open for the season. The summer season in 1866 looked bleak for Saratoga with two big hotels closed. There were very real prospects that failure to find rooms would result in Saratoga's patrons discovering alternative venues and not returning. Understanding the need to rebuild, the Hathorns (740 Br), who owned Congress Hall, set about rebuilding immediately. Freeburn was employed by Hathorn as a mason to set the foundation for the "new" Congress Hotel. It was during the reconstruction that he is credited with discovering what would be named the Hathorn Spring.

After Freeborn died, one of his daughters and her family moved into the house to take care of his widow. The daughter, Eliza, was the wife of Lewis B. Hays, a second generation confectioner and wholesaler. Although Hays' store was the local candy shop, the bulk of this business was from his production of candy for the wholesale market. Hays' business was at 425 Broadway in what was called surprisingly enough the Hays Building. The building was damaged in a fire in 1905 but rebuilt.

The Hays family, including their daughter Margaret, lived in the house for over 60 years. The years overlapped with Freeborn's because the two families lived together for a period. Margaret became the Home Economics teacher at Saratoga High School (now Lake Ave). In the 1930s when her family was gone she sold the house and moved 96 Lake Avenue to be nearer her work.

After she had retired Margaret was interviewed regarding her memories of Saratoga. She related the story of how when she was a young girl one of her playmates was Charles Brackett (605 Br). While sitting on his back porch the two children would watch as Lillian Russell and Diamond Jim Brady had breakfast together at 22 Greenfield. This is best proof we have of where Lillian Russell actually stayed.

BROADWAY

588

Hanson

The union of Aimee Lathrop and Walter Hanson was to be one of the best examples ever of the expression, "where the wheel meets the road."

As a member of the firm Thatcher & Lathrop Aimee's father, Daniel Lathrop, had made a fortune manufacturing the steel wheels used on all forms of railroad cars. Walter's father, Henry Hanson, who classified himself a capitalist, had made his own fortune constructing railroad lines across this country and in Canada. The senior Hanson was responsible for the construction of such railroad lines as the Long Island RR; Louisville, Evanston & St. Louis RR; and locally the Albany & Troy RR and the Johnstown & Gloversville RR. In his later years Henry Hanson retired, lived full time in Saratoga and invested in coal mines in both British Columbia and Kentucky.

After Aimee's father died in 1883, the Lathrop family elected to leave their home in Albany and reside full time at *Annandale* one of the biggest houses in the village (245 Clinton at the corner of Clement). If not the wealthiest family in the village, the Lathrops, were clearly in the top ten. It had been reported that Aimee and her two sisters were each expected to inherit five million dollars.

Hanson's parents lived at 75 Clinton, the corner of Walden. It could be said by those just looking at the two Clinton Street addresses that the two families lived just down the street from each other. However, their parents' grand cottages were separated by more than just space; the houses in-between lacked the grandeur of the two families' estates.

Wedding

Their marriage, in March of 1889, was the merger of two of the wealthiest families in the village. Although the wedding was early in March everyone that was there knew it would be one of the biggest events in Saratoga that year. This wedding was supposed to be the fairy-tale where the woman known as "Miss Benevolent" and one of the handsomest young men in the village would commit themselves to each other.

Although it was March, the month of blizzards in Upstate New York, even Mother Nature knew better than to mess with Mrs. Harriet Lathrop. The weather conditions the evening of their union were described as close to perfect.

The First Presbyterian Church (which stood between the Collamer and Algonquin Buildings) had been decorated as rarely before. Electric lights had been installed for the occasion. To symbolize hope, florist T. J. Totten (158 Lake) had used white flowers to create a large white dove which was suspended over the wedding party. To create an atmosphere that symbolized the binding together of the two people Totten had covered vines with flowers. The vines were attached to a large wedding bell in the center of the church extending over the pews and down the side walls of the church. The alter had been decorated with imported tropical plants.

The list of invited guest looked like the index for this series. There were so many people who had received invitations that it would take the better part of an hour for the eight ushers to seat everyone. To entertain those who arrived in a timely manner, an orchestra had been brought in from Troy. Locals who knew either the bride or groom but did have invitations crowed against each other along the side walls and in the back. To those in the village this was hardly an event to miss.

There were far too many people present to fit in the church. Those who could not gain admission lined Broadway waiting patiently to see how the wedding party and guests were dressed. They were not disappointed.

The bride was like a local princess arriving in a carriage pulled by a span of chestnut horses. As the carriage turned onto the street Aimee was greeted by what could only be portrayed as throngs of well-wishers. Her serenity and treatment of others was so well known in the village that some of the urchins felt comfortable climbing up on the carriage to wish her their best. Their fathers and older brothers climbed onto the driver's seat and even on to the backs of the horses to cheer her on. She, in her own way, was a cross between the social heroin and the conscience of the village.

When she descended from the carriage she stood before the throng dressed in a white satin dress the skirt of which was covered in delicate lace. She wore all the diamonds and other precious jewels that could be worn without appearing pretentious. She was after all so widely esteemed that she was capable of going anywhere without fear of robbery.

The one truly unique twist was who accompanied the bride as she walked down the isle. Having no brothers and with her father deceased, it would have been customary to have an uncle or cousin as an escort. Her mother's brother was Leland Stanford, who, at the time of the wedding, was the Senator from California. He had previously been the head of the Central Pacific Railroad and the Governor of California. As one of the richest men in America, he would have been the perfect escort for such an occasion. Instead Aimee Lathrop was escorted down the isle by her mother, Harriet, who wore black satin and no jewelry. The severity of Harriet's dress was not necessary as she had been a widow for two years.

Throughout the ceremony there was soft music playing while the priest conducted the marriage ritual. When the wedding was over the invited quests boarded carriages and proceeded to the reception at *Annandale*.

In the custom of the day the presents had all been sent in advance. A guard had been placed at the door of one of the upstairs rooms at *Annandale*. He was placed there so the guests could see the treasure of gifts but would be sure they did not become tempted to share in the bounty. In a crowd such as those invited, the guard was largely ceremonial.

The couple had announced they were going to Europe for their honeymoon. Knowing that some of his friends enjoyed wedding pranks the couple feared antics at the train station. The couple escaped for their honeymoon by catching the midnight train at a station out of town. Everyone in the village was made aware of their departure when six torpedoes went off. The couple fooled any who planned later pranks when they went to Japan not Europe as had been leaked.

Those with a romantic nature would have expected such a ceremony to foretell of a storybook relationship; such was not the case.

Bankruptcy
Frugal was not a trait the young Hansons would list on their resume. Around 1898, Walter accepted a position in New York City

working as a broker. The couple continued to reside in Saratoga but took a second residence in Brooklyn. It appears Hanson liked to invest in highly speculative ventures.

In April of 1900 the couple declared bankruptcy in Federal Court in Utica. The location was picked to help reduce the local notoriety. Since each expected to inherit a significant fortune within the decade, they both knew their financial difficulties were only temporary.

1905 a big year

In 1905, Aimee's aunt, Jane Stanford, the widow of Leland, one of the wealthiest men in America, died in Hawaii. She had gone to the islands to recover from an attempt on her life; someone had tried to poison her in California. There were rumors, which persist to this day, that her death was the result of strychnine poison.

Although Jane's husband, Leland Stanford, had left twenty million to Stanford University, there was still an estimated thirty million left for his widow ($400,000,000 and $600,000,000 in today's dollars respectively). The Stanford's only son had died years before on a trip to Italy. Aimee, her sister, a niece and nephew and Stanford University were to be the recipients of the family's fortune.

The same year Henry Hanson, Walter's father, died in Saratoga. Suddenly Aimee and Walter's money problems were a thing of the past.

Lost

The first three decades of the last century was a period when people tried to set all kinds of records. Records were regularly printed for such things as distances flown nonstop, travel by bicycle in a single day, automobile speed and distance, and even train speeds. Establishing a record, any record, was all the rage.

Although their son Walter Lathrop Hanson was planning to attend college in the fall of 1909, he had not been feeling well for some time and was losing weight. His parents, Walter Hedrick and Aimee decided that rather than college a family adventure might be the exact prescription needed to expedite their son's recovery. To get fresh air they decided on a cross country car trip.

At the time of the Hanson family's excursion autos were still a relatively new and an undependable form of transportation. Since autos broke down and had flat tires regularly, cars were used almost exclusively within the owner's community. Four years before there had only been 250 cars in all of Saratoga and many of those were for rent not owned by individuals.

To add to the Hanson's adventure the number of miles of paved roads in cities was limited. In rural America there were no paved roads. Cross country expeditions, like they planned, were over dirt roads full of deep ruts, huge puddles and sharp stones. None of which were good for the fragile tires.

On November 28th, the Hanson family and their chauffer left Saratoga to travel cross country by automobile. If successful, the Hansons would be the first to make a cross continent trip via the southern route. The legs of their trip were: New York City (placing them on one coast), Washington D.C., Richmond, Atlanta, New Orleans, San Antonio, El Paso, Tucson, Phoenix, and finally Los Angles (the other coast). They would continue to San Francisco but that was after they had already completed the cross country objective.

In part the trip was for business. Walter told friends he visited in each of the cities that on the trip that he had backing from Wall Street and was looking with "interest into several deals." By mid-February 1910, the family had reached Phoenix. The trip had all the markings of success with young Walter having already put on twenty pounds.

When they got to Phoenix there had only been two tight spots on the trip, both occurred on rural roads in Louisiana. For over 300 miles in the Bayou and Lone Star States they drove through mud so deep they rarely left first gear. In the middle of a low muddy flatland of Louisiana, the Hansons were confronted by a group of forward thinking farmers who considered automobiles a noisy nuisance. The rednecks had used their wagons to block the road, insisting the Hansons turn around. Not the kind of man to be dissuaded from his mission Walter Hanson got into an argument with the farmers. When the locals produced their assorted rifles and shotguns, Walter elected to turn his car around.

Returning to the last village they had traveled through, Hanson sought out the local sheriff. Provided with a posse on horseback, the Hansons were escorted back down the same road to finish that leg of their trip. There was no record of the size of the contribution Hanson made to the sheriff's retirement fund for the support of the posse.

Their trip took them through very rural areas. Each time the Hansons stopped for a break in New Mexico and Arizona they would return to the car to find it surrounded by Native Americans who had never seen an automobile before.

In Phoenix the Hansons were surprised to meet several people from Saratoga who had gone to the dessert for the winter. While visiting with their neighbors the adventurers were warned about the dangers of trying to cross the unfamiliar desert that lay ahead. They trusted the skills and judgment of their chauffer who had been with them for 12 years; nevertheless the Hansons decided to hire an experienced guide for the final leg of their trip. Unfortunately, the man they wanted was at the other side of the desert. They sent a telegraph but it took four days to find the guide and get him to Phoenix by train.

After spending exactly a week in Phoenix, the Hanson party set out for Mecca, California. The desert they were going to cross had rarely been seen from the seat of a motorized vehicle. They were seen crossing the Colorado River then went missing during a sand storm in the California desert. The wind was so fierce that it tore the flaps from the sides of the car. The first day they were late people were not overly concerned. When they were two days overdue associates in Mecca sent a car out into the desert in search of the missing party. The search car returned without making a sighting. As night set in another car was being outfitted for a second search. Unannounced the Hanson party arrived in the hamlet. They only had a half a gallon of gas to spare. Even with the guide the storm had been so severe that they had gotten lost going many miles off course.

Undeterred by their adventures in the desert, the Hanson family continued on. The final leg of their trip was following the Pacific coast from Los Angles to San Francisco. One of the most amazing parts of the trip which ended in April, six months after it began, is that it was completed without a single even minor issue with the Stearns Touring Car.

One life ends; a relationship changes

Saratogians were shocked in January of 1912 when the headlines read that Walter H. Hanson (father) had died at his Brooklyn residence. The cause of death was listed as Bright's Disease a term that covered a multitude of kidney illnesses. He had symptoms for several years but had recovered from all the previous attacks. Even this attack was thought to have been cured by a recent trip to Atlantic City.

In the years between his marriage and death Hanson had been active in Saratoga politics and the Masonic order. He had served as a village trustee and had even been considered for the position of president of the village. He had been a force for the reform politics of 1894. Over the ensuing decade he had had a change of party and in November of 1911 he had been the Democratic candidate for State Assembly representing Saratoga.

He was laid to rest in the family mausoleum in Greenridge Cemetery. Although they had had issues between mother and son for a while, Walter's death would trigger a set of events that would rip the two apart.

Aimee knew her son and his lack of responsibility, possibly even better than his father. Before the funeral was over Aimee engaged Nash Rockwood (31 Union) and had him draw up a letter of assignment whereby her son's share of his father's estate would be cared for by her. According to the son on the day after his father's funeral he went to Rockwood's Saratoga office and signed the letter of assignment with the assumption that he would receive a yearly allowance and the remainder of his share of his father's estate when he was ready to go into business for himself. He would later say that his mother threatened him with insanity proceedings if he did not sign the letter. When her son put his name on the paper, Aimee had won the first round.

Whether because of his father's death; drinking to excess; or other emotional issues the following twelve months would be disastrous for Walter Lathrop Hanson (son). The time would not be much better for his mother. He was drinking heavily. He started to give away objects or sell them for a fraction of their value. He tried to sell his mother's $2,700 auto for $50; he sold a $100 diamond stickpin for $3. More damaging was when he broke into his mother's desk and took the key to her safe deposit box. Popular and persuasive he was able to convince the teller that he had permission to enter the box. He took several of his mother's pins which he traded to young ladies for casual favors. His problems became so serious that his mother had him admitted to the McCarthy Institute (1 Broadway) to dry out. Aimee also claimed that during the same period he had engaged in orgies in Philadelphia and Chester, PA.

To really add to the mix, in November of the same year Walter married Henriette Reutti, a singer in one of the vaudeville shows in Harlem. It was the final straw; Aimee cut off Walter's allowance. Beautiful and cunning Reutti and Aimee would match stares in more than one courtroom.

Two suits started in 1913. Aimee Hanson went to court to have her son declared incompetent. Walter sued to get control of the money he had been left by his father. The first issue was where the family resided; he claimed he lived in Brooklyn (a place less controlled by his mother and Rockwood); his mother admitted they had a residence in Brooklyn but claimed they lived in Saratoga. It was settled that the family lived in Saratoga.

The appropriate venue decided the court also upheld the document creating the trust.

Having not been able to get his mother to agree to allow him access to his portion of this father's estate, Walter told his mother that he was going to return to his wife. Instead he left the country and was in Canada when in May of 1913 the competency suit filed by his mother reached the judge. It was held that he was a habitual drinker and unable to manage his money. The court provided a group of trustees to administer his father's estate.

For Walter and Reutti the issue with his mother needed to be fought as much in the media as in the courtroom. It was claimed that Reutti had made an unsuccessful return to the stage following the marriage. Walter to show his suffering would be sure that a story was released to the effect that to offset the legal cost, Reutti, had taken a position working in mill; of course he refused to name the mill. He claimed he was helping meet expenses working as a car salesperson.

The battle between mother and son would rage for three years. Finally in 1916 two separate actions were initiated. Reutti filed charges against Aimee for alienation of affection, a charged no longer allowed in New York State. Reutti's claim was based on Walter's leaving her in May of 1913. Reutti would hold that he only did so because his mother had insisted he leave her or she would continue to cut off his allowance. By this time Walter was working as a chauffer in San Diego. He again filed suit to get control of the money his father had left.

Aimee's attorney, Nash Rockwood, was relishing getting Walter on the stand and under oath. His reasons were comments made by Walter in his affidavit. Walter held that he was taught to gamble by his parents. He went on to say that his parents had always permitted him to drink, even as a child. In his mind the implication was simple: they taught him to play; they had an obligation to pay.

To show how far he had slipped he added that his father had not died of any illness but rather as the result of having been hit on the head by a blackjack. In his affidavit he also claimed it was his father who had pawned the jewels in question not himself. Walter went on to say that his mother threatened to have him kidnapped. It should be noted that he never said why his father needed to pawn the jewels; where his father was when he was knocked unconscious or why his mother would want him kidnapped.

The issues would not be dragged into a courtroom for two years. Finally in October of 1918 the case of Hanson vs. Hanson for alienation of affections finally came before a jury. Reutti was seeking $100,000 in damages.

Walter's testimony was essential to Reutti's case, since he was the only one who could tell why his feelings for her had changed. Unfortunately for Reutti the trial came about at the same time as the Spanish Influenza. Walter who was living in Santa Anna, California came down with the flu the last week of October. He only suffered for four days. When it became apparent he was dying Walter gave an affidavit in California on behalf of his wife, even though they were not living together.

It took five days for the body, accompanied by floral tributes, to be transported to Saratoga. Before the trial could resume, Rockwood moved for adjournment so that Aimee could attend her son's funeral. Aimee had moved for adjournment first and Reutti missed the opportunity to play the sympathy card.

Walter was laid to rest in the same mausoleum as his father; however, the newspapers barely noticed. It was November 7, 1918, and peace talks were on to end the First World War.

In general the newspapers felt that Reutti was coming off as someone who wanted revenge not someone seeking justice.

The 1920 census lists Aimee Hanson as living in the Hamptons and her profession was that of operating a duck farm.

In August of 1954, Aimee Lathrop Hanson died at her home in Westhampton Beach, Long Island. She was the last surviving woman from the group that founded Saratoga Hospital. She was nearly ninety and found herself without family. She was laid to rest in the Hanson Lathrop Mausoleum in Greenridge Cemetery.

She was with her son and her husband; the feuds within the family were finally laid to rest.

BROADWAY

590

Slocum

For many years this little house, nestled among its imposing neighbors, belonged to William Slocum. His life as a farmer did not seem to have been injurious to his health, since Slocum was 89 when he died in 1893. Slocum had been a village trustee in the 1860s. His son, Henry Slocum, was a Methodist minister.

Following Slocum's death the house had several short-term residents including the director of the summer theater, a young lawyer, and a widow. Finally, in 1905, Ransom Qua adopted the house.

While Qua lived in the house the population of Saratoga had not yet reached 15,000. There is an expression that in a small community all businesses have to offer more than one service. Qua owned one of the more unusual combinations in the village. He was a coal dealer and had a grocery store at the same Lake Avenue address. One has to hope that the there was enough space to keep the two operations separate.

Qua had served in the 123rd New York Volunteers (the Washington County company). He enlisted as a private in the company raised in Hartford and Hebron. His military career was skyrocketed when he was promoted to corporal in March 1865. Qua was 77 when he died in 1917.

The house is clearly in two parts. The earlier part is brick and the addition is the shingle area on the north side, probably added after Slocum owned the house.

BROADWAY

595

Pettee

He told his secretary and his wife that he was going on a business trip to visit his facility in Virginia. He went on to say that he expected to be back in a couple of days. Since he had taken many similar trips, no one thought it peculiar until it was learned two days later that he never showed up at the Virginia operation.

It was May of 1923 and newspapers across the country were treated to the brand of scandal on which they thrive. Headlines similar to the one in the *Saratogian;* **Pettee Gone; $300,000 Missing**; or the one the following day in the *New York Times;* **Vanishes Leaving $300,000 Shortage** ran in newspapers across the country. Whatever the headline, the fact was simple the person who had built this house the year before was one of the most famous missing persons in the country.

In response to the news both the national press telegraphs were sending out his picture and description. Not surprisingly there were suddenly "Pettee sightings" everywhere especially in Saratoga.

***

Lore has it that the man who built this house was the mayor who embezzled the city's money and disappeared. Like much that is passed along as oral history, this is the merger of two separate accounts blended together to make a more appealing tale.

Unfortunately for the storytellers, the truth concerning the events is a little different. Pettee had been the mayor of Saratoga from 1917-1919. It is also true that he embezzled $300,000. The problem for the storytellers is that his term as mayor had been over for four years when the embezzlement occurred. In fact the money that was taken was from his company, not the city. However, since

109

so many local citizens invested in Pettee's company, it probably felt to many of them that the missing money was from the city's coffers.

Harry Pettee, with his brother, George, started a company bottling the carbon dioxide that was present in the springs out near the Geysers (see Natural Gas). His company, General Carbonic Gas, grew quickly and by 1911 he was in a position to buy the house at 55 Union Avenue. Handsome, likable and at the least financially comfortable, Pettee was immensely popular in the city. In 1916 he decided to turn his popularity into politics running successfully for mayor. The spread in the popular vote in his victory was a larger than any of the other successful candidates.

Pettee's gas company was one of those that had been caught up in the State's efforts to save the springs by banning the bottling of carbon dioxide. By the end of the first decade in the century it was understood that the underground carbon dioxide gas was needed as pressure to force the spring water to the surface. By an act of the State Legislature in the early teens, Pettee was forced to sell his company's holdings in the area of the geysers.

***

From the record it seems that the money Pettee received for his gas rights changed his standard of living or at least his attitude on spending. Forced out of Saratoga, Pettee moved his principal operations to Newark, New Jersey and Long Island City, while making his headquarters in Manhattan. Over the next five years Pettee's gas company expanded to include seven different gas bottling plants around the country.

In 1923 Pettee's salary as president of the company was $25,000 a year (at least 20 times that of the average worker). The dividends on his stock holdings had been in the vicinity of another $40,000 each year. In total it was estimated that in the three years before his disappearance his total compensation had exceeded $200,000. If the reported $300,000 was missing, the natural question became where did the $500,000 go? To add to the dilemma it was learned that in the days before he disappeared Pettee had his wife sign over an insurance policy she owned so that he could cash it in, providing him with another $15,000.

With no history of gambling or drinking to excess, the reporters started looking into his lifestyle. It was soon learned that he enjoyed spending several weeks each winter in Palm Beach. His trips south were so frequent that while he was mayor of Saratoga he was given the dubious nickname of "Palm Beach going Mayor." At the time of the embezzlement Pettee and his wife maintained an apartment in New York City, the island of conspicuous consumption. Even measured against those who lived well he was considered a "spender."

The answer to the disappearing money was discovered in the three rambling notes that Pettee left behind in the company safe. He admitted that he had been "inappropriately intimate" with a female whose name he wrote in the note but was never released to the media. In the notes he mentioned suicide by jumping off an ocean going ship, but no one except his wife thought him capable of taking his own life (she may have been hoping).

What is known is that the women mentioned in the notes remained in New York City; that he did not have a passport to board a foreign vessel; that his wife kept their Saratoga home for a decade; and that Harry was never seen again.

***

There is a second story that deserves close examination. Could it be that he was so angry with the city that when his wife pushed for this house to be built he literally turned his back on the city? – This house is built backward - the pillars and porches are on the back.

BROADWAY

596

Captain Butler

This house was owned by the politically active Butler family for over sixty years. First owned by Captain James Prentiss Butler, he would leave it to his wife and daughter. His son Walter, a lawyer like his father, established a home of his own.

Captain James Butler was born in 1816 in Essex County where he studied law becoming the district attorney. In 1857 he moved to Saratoga and changed sides of the courtroom, setting up practice as a criminal attorney. Captain Butler was one of the leading attorneys in the defense of the wealthy Jesse Billings for the murder of his wife (there were two trials; the first resulted in a hung jury; in the second Billings was found not guilty). One of Billings' key witnesses was a fisherman named Jones. After the first trial, Jones was charged with perjury. Butler led Jones' defense. In a bizarre twist of events Jones was found guilty and Billings innocent (see *To Spend Eternity Alone*).

James was forty-five when the Civil War broke out. Considering himself too old for service, he still felt the need to serve the Union. At his own expense James went to Washington D. C. and served for ten days as a guard at the White House. In April of 1863, he was appointed Provost Marshal of this region. He would recruit the first "colored soldiers." Unlike other states, the soldiers Butler recruited would serve beside their white counterparts not in separate divisions. James' son was born during the war. James paid a bounty on behalf of his infant son, Walter and a soldier was recruited in his place. The soldier died in battle and because the soldier was a replacement, Walter was listed as a casualty in the war.

James remained active in politics serving as a village trustee for four years and a county supervisor for two years. Butler's two children were Walter and Allena.

After James died in 1894, Allena, stayed in the house and cared for her mother for several decades. When she was in her fifties she would marry for the first time. Her husband was Orton Brown (649 Br).

Walter had all the privileges of money. He attended the best private schools including Phillips-Exeter Academy and Columbia Law School. In addition to earning three athletic letters at Phillips-Exeter, Walter was sportsman enjoying hunting, fishing and camping. He was one of the best golfers at both the Saratoga Golf Club and McGregor Links.

In 1903 Walter had the distinction of owning the second automobile in the city; a one cylinder Oldsmobile. Walter would have another driving distinction for several years he would be the first driver to reach New York City from Saratoga in the spring.

Like his father Walter was active in social and political causes. He was active in the Red Cross for over twenty years. When Saratoga became a city in 1915 Walter was elected the first Mayor. He was also the President of the First National Bank.

Unlike his father most of Walter's law practice was civil. His earliest partner was Edgar Brackett (605 Br). A large part of Walter's case work involved inheritance taxes; however, he also represented the local Vichy Company in a case that went to the U. S. Supreme Court. The local bottling company was sued by the Republic of France who wanted them to cease their use of the name Vichy claiming a conflict with the original city. Butler and the Vichy Company won the case.

Walter and his wife, Mary Kilmer (722 Br), resided at 22 Greenfield. In the 1890s they rented their house to Diamond Jim Brady and Lillian Russell while they traveled during the season. One year they took a trip to Europe.

BROADWAY

598

Captain Bogert

This house was built in 1883 for a former sea captain, David Bogert. Captain Bogert had spent his life aboard ships that traded along the east coast. This house would be lived in for fifty years by the captain's daughters, Elizabeth and Katherine. The sisters were what was referred to at the time as "genteel women"; members of a class in society that has been virtually lost. The sisters never married or worked having been provided for by their father.

The term "genteel woman" usually referred to a single female who was born into a middle class or higher family. Her parents at some point had come to understand that she would probably never marry. Since she would not have anyone to "care for her," her financial security depended on her parents. Before Social Security, the genteel daughter was often raised to be the caretaker of her parents when they aged.

According to the customs of the highly ordered Victorian Society, genteel women were expected to adhere to the strictest set of rules. They could never be seen alone in the company of a man other than family members; they could only do charitable work, collecting food for the poor and sewing for soldiers. Their's was a life based on structure, not pleasure.

Elizabeth, the younger of the two, would die in 1924; Catherine would live to be eighty, dying in 1930. The sisters' influence and acceptance of the rules can be understood by looking at who was selected as bearers at their funeral. The men chosen were from the leading families in what was, by that time, the city; included in the group were the president of a bank and the district attorney.

BROADWAY

601

Travers
Janvrin
Pardue
Houghton

One house, four owners, each of whom deserves to be noted.

This house was built for one of the most popular stock brokers in history (almost an oxymoron). He was a man who, despite a serious speech impediment, was known for his great sense of humor. He was a man who came close to losing his fortune at least twice, yet ended on top. He was also the man who lent his name to Saratoga Race Track's most famous stakes race. Born in Baltimore he was educated in schools in New York City. He was a member of 27 clubs, at the time of his death in 1887.

The *New York Times* reported that William R. Travers was considered one of the most popular men in the City; of course, what the newspaper failed to mention was that he was in Bermuda, not the city when he died.

With the exception of his horse named Kentucky, the winner of the first Travers' Stakes, Travers association horse racing was more for ownership of the tracks than from the horses. For a time, Travers owned the Saratoga Race Track in a partnership with the famous pugilist John Morrissey. The two had a falling out and Travers elected to sell his share of the track. Until the time of his death, he would continue to own Jerome Park, which he leased to the New York Racing Association. Returning to his native Baltimore each spring, he usually attended the racing meet at Pimlico even after he had stopped coming to Saratoga.

Although he never gave up his love of horses, Travers also loved sailing. Since he no longer owned the Saratoga track he started spending the "season" in Newport where he built himself a cottage to replace this one. In 1876 he had built a 72 foot sloop named the *Fanny* which he captained in many successful races. His health beginning to fail from diabetes, Travers sold the yacht in 1883 to the partner of one of his sons-in-laws.

The size of the house may in part be attributed to need; Travers had three sons and five daughters. Like all parents with a flock this size, some were more successful than others. His two oldest sons became partners in brokerage houses in New York City. His third son added color to the family portrait when in 1885 a Miss Sadie McNeil of Brooklyn claimed to be secretly married to one of the Travers boys. The *Times* immediately dispatched a reporter to trace the story. Meeting Sadie at the door to her house, the reporter took the liberty of describing the blonde Scottish lass as "pretty, plump and positive." She refused to comment at length but did show her ring and say she was married to Reverdy Travers. The story came out that she and Reverdy had married and he lived with her a couple of weeks in the spring, then went to the family's summer home in Newport to enjoy the season. When William heard of his son's adventure there was a confrontation. The one thing that is known about the outcome is that Reverdy and Sadie went to Europe on their honeymoon the next week.

When Travers started spending the season in Newport, he sold this house to Louis Janvrin. As James Marvin (3 FS) was aging, he started to step back from the daily operations of the United States Hotel on Division Street. To assure that the hotel's reputation would remain intact, Marvin recruited Louis Janvrin to work with his son-in-law and nephew-in-law as manager of the hotel. Janvrin became what today would be considered general manager. Janvrin had experience having been the proprietor of the Fifth Avenue Hotel in New York City. After 14 years operating the United States Hotel, Janvrin had a stroke in the year 1891. He died Dec. 8, 1892 of paralysis; he was only 52 at the time. His wife, two sons and a daughter remained in the house for two years after he died then moved to apartments in the Pardue building (now the Algonquin).

The next resident was a merchant named James Pardue. Pardue opened and operated a store named the China Hall. The store which was obviously very successful was in the Pardue Building (The Algonquin). The business sold exactly the type of products one would have expected, specializing in china, lamps, Queensware, and knickknacks. Many of the people who came to Saratoga were the first members of their family to ever be on vacation. It was almost imperative that they have a souvenir that they could display at home that would show they had been away. Pardue products were evidence that they had been in the city.

Although it was common to make a significant profit from all the visitors anxious to purchase a souvenir, Pardue took profit a step further by avoiding purchasing from importers and buying directly from dealers in China and Japan.

It was the fourth resident that added the most dignity to the house. Justice James Houghton was made of the same fabric as his contemporary, Teddy Roosevelt. Born on a farm in Corinth, at age 13 Houghton's father died. The oldest boy in a family of seven children, he wanted to reduce his mother's expenses and went to live with his aunt on her farm in Canandaigua, New York. For the rest of his life he attributed his health and "sturdy constitution" to the manual labor he performed on his aunt's farm. More important to him was the quality of the school in his aunt's village. At fifteen, an age when most boys were leaving school, Houghton started at Canandaigua Academy. Because he had to work on the farm, he was 20 before he finished high school. Although he would regret it for the rest of his life, Houghton did not attend college. After graduation Houghton immediately started reading for the law and was admitted to the bar in Rochester in 1879.

Houghton then returned to Saratoga where he began the practice of law. Although accepting his role as a community leader, Houghton's entry into politics was slower than most men who would become judges. His first office was in 1887 when he became a member of the Board of Police Commissioners.

It was what happened to Houghton in 1888 that is one of the best examples of a dark horse winning a race that no one ever expected him to enter. At the Republican's county convention in Ballston, it took 62 ballots to select the candidate for county judge. The issue was not Houghton; it was the conflict between the other, more senior lawyers who sought the position. Houghton was finally selected as a compromise candidate. His greatest attribute was who he had not angered, more than his own record – it was too short. Eleven years and two successful elections later, Houghton was appointed by then Governor Teddy Roosevelt to New York State Supreme Court. Later he would become a judge in the Third Department of the Court of Appeals.

Living on a farm in his youth created a love of the outdoors that he carried with him throughout his life. He always looked fit, so his friends were surprised when in the winter of 1913, and just before his 57th birthday, he traveled to Boston to check himself into a private hospital. The hospital he chose was where his son practiced. A few days after his arrival, Houghton was successfully operated on for appendicitis. During his recovery the judge contracted pneumonia and died within days.

Mrs. Houghton was so shocked by the events relating to her husband's death that her health immediately started to fail. Six months after her husband's death she had two strokes within one weekend. The second was fatal.

BROADWAY

604

The Orphan

Two of the great questions are: when is a house not a home? And when is a house an orphan? For almost two decades in the early 1880s through the turn of the last century this house either had no resident or the residents were temporary. The absence was so serious that according to the village directories there was a period of five years when no one occupied the house. In 1903 that changed when Henrietta Cramer of Troy started using the house as a summer residence. She would continue to use the house during the season for a decade and a half.

In the 1880s the house had been occasionally occupied. One of the first tenants was the Reverend Peter Stryker, the priest at the First Presbyterian Church on Broadway. He was very unique in listing his children as residents; most listings were just the head of the family. He would leave the church and village in 1884. Vacant for three years Horace Ruggles, a lawyer from New York City, rented the house in the summer for three seasons. The house then languished with no one living there for at least five years.

The cost to rent had dropped so much that by 1899, Mrs. Mary McCall was renting her house on Circular Street for the season and staying in this house. Finally, in 1904 Mrs. Cramer started her long run in the house during the season.

Mrs. Cramer was replaced by Mrs. Katie Farnham, who would reside in the house for the next thirty years. Mrs. Farnham's husband, George, had been the proprietor of the American and Adelphi Hotels.

BROADWAY

605

Brackett

There are parallel questions which can be continuously asked: Which is more significant? The affect Saratoga has on its people or the affect its people have had on Saratoga? Two generations of the Brackett family lived in this house during its first forty years. The members of those generations are a classic example of why the questions will never be fully answered. The father, who adopted the village, had a remarkable impact on Saratoga; while the son, who grew up in the house then moved away, had a *dramatic* effect on one of America's *premier* industries.

Edgar Brackett, the first generation, was born in Wilton in 1853; however, while he was still a boy his family moved to Iowa. He resided in the Midwest until 1872, the year he graduated from Cornell College of Iowa. Immediately after college, Brackett moved to Saratoga where he commenced the study of law in the office of Pond and French (718 Br). Admitted to the bar in 1875, the following year he became a partner and the firm was renamed Pond, French and Brackett.

The origin of Brackett's early money is not easy to ascertain. We do know that when he was only 32 years old (1885) he was living in this "Great Lady." One source may have been through his marriage in 1883 to Emma Corliss of Providence, Rhode Island. Emma's father, Charles, was associated with the Corliss Steam Engine company. The Corliss Company had designed and built the engine that powered the entire 1876 World's Fair in Philadelphia. The Corliss Mansion in Providence, which their son would inherit, is now part of Brown University.

Several of Edgar Brackett's investments would have carried the family for generations had it not been for his son's personal success and not needing any inheritance. In 1890, Brackett was one of the initial investors in G. F. Harvey Company. In 1900, along with some associates, he founded the Adirondack Trust Company. He served as president for the first quarter century of the bank's existence. He also invested in Iroquois Paper Company outside Schuylerville and the Hudson Paper Company. For many people of Saratoga it was his development of the McGregor Country Club for which he is most appreciated.

Brackett should be remembered for his political impact even more than his financial achievements. In 1895 he was elected to the New York State Senate as a Reform Republican. He served from 1896 – 1906 and again from 1908 – 1912. While in the Senate he worked tirelessly to break up the system in which too much power was in the hands of the leadership. One only has to look at how the Senate and Assembly operate today to see that his energy was virtually wasted. Brackett was also a fighter to regulate the insurance business, which at the time made much of its money by refusing to pay claims. By 1904 Brackett was so well recognized statewide that he was nominated as the Republican candidate for Governor. Unsuccessful on behalf of himself, Brackett was never-the-less influential behind the scene. Two years later, when Charles Hughes successfully ran for Governor, Brackett had been in charge of the campaign. Brackett was a true politician claiming among his personal friends such people as Presidents Taft and Harding.

With Brackett's support Charles Hughes would later hold many national offices including: Secretary of State, Chief Justice of the Supreme Court and Republican candidate for President in 1916.

Brackett's political ideas on behalf of Saratoga had both positive and negative impacts. In the mid 1890s there was a move by a group of Saratogians to end the gambling that was so openly practiced in the city. Brackett was one of the biggest supporters of those in the city who attempted to eliminate gambling. Unlike some of the other participants in the reform, Brackett was able to survive the political reaction that followed. In the election of 1896, literally the entire reform slate was defeated, yet Brackett won a seat in the State Senate.

On the positive side Brackett led two legislative actions that proved beneficial to the city. Brackett initiated legislation that ended the practice of extracting the carbon dioxide gas from the spring water. His actions contributed to saving the springs that were still producing. The legislation required the State to pay the fair market price for the land on which the gas bottling plants were operating. A true politician, Brackett then represented the gas producers in court in an attempt to increase the value of their holdings. The outcome was more for the few who owned the land at the expense of the taxpayers. In later years Brackett would be the president of Star Gas Company, one of the businesses the State bought out, which had relocated out of the area.

Toward the end of his service as a senator, in 1909, Brackett introduced legislation that led to the creation of the State Reservation which would grow to include the Gideon Putnam, two golf courses, and SPAC. For his efforts he is called "The Father of the State Reservation."

Brackett was not without his enemies. When the reform ticket won in 1895, the village president, Caleb Mitchell (149 Ph), was removed from office because Mitchell's resort was one of the gambling halls. By 1903 Mitchell was a broken man. One morning he went to Brackett's law office in City Hall and asked for a meeting. Learning that Brackett was not expected in that day, Mitchell went into the center hall and shot himself in the head. It was felt by many that Mitchell's intention was to first shoot Brackett then himself.

Brackett was also selected as the successful manager (prosecutor) of the impeachment case against Governor Shulz.

The Bracketts had two sons, Edgar junior and Charles. When Edgar was nine he was playing with a pistol loaded with blank cartridges. Since there was no projectile, the powder of the blank was held in the by wadding. When he fired the gun in the direction of his foot some of the wadding broke the skin. Three days later young Edgar died of tetanus. In memory of their son, the Bracketts paid for an addition to Saratoga Hospital. Later, Brackett gave an organ to the Methodist Church that was reported in 1921 to cost $50,000. The other beneficiary of his philanthropy was Skidmore College.

Brackett's remaining son, Charles, grew up in the house. He attended the public high school before matriculating at Williams College. He went on to get his law degree from Harvard. Returning to Saratoga, Charles became a member of the law firm of Brackett, Eddy, & Dorsey.

During World War I, Charles served as assistant liaison officer to Gen. Contonceau in France. He was decorated by the French government with the Medaille d'Honneur in Argent.

Charles was more interested in writing than the practice of law. He wrote several books including: <u>Counsel of the Ungodly</u>

(1920); <u>The Last Infirmity</u> (1925); and <u>American Colony</u> (1929). He wrote articles that appeared in magazines such as the *Saturday Evening Post* and *Colliers*. From 1925 until 1929 Brackett was the drama critic for the *New Yorker*. With a flair for adventure Brackett began writing screen plays with his first credit in 1925. In the mid 1930s movies had dialog and Brackett signed a contract with Paramount Studios as a screen-writer. His success came when he partnered with Billie Wilder. Wilder was a hard living personality while Brackett was content spending his evenings smoking a cigar and playing cards. Although their relationship was strained, the two would work together on at least 13 movies. Arguably the most famous collaboration being *Sunset Boulevard* (1950) starring Gloria Swanson, for which they both won the Oscar for Best Screen Writing. Eventually Brackett would be known as both a writer and producer; earning a second Oscar for his 1953 movie *Titanic*. Brackett was the president of the Screen Actors Guild (1938) and the Academy of Motion Picture Arts and Sciences from 1949 – 55.

It is his screenplays for which he is famous. Among those still seen today were: The *Lost Weekend* (1945); *The Last Infirmity*; *Entirely Surrounded* and *Counsel of the Ungodly*. Along with Billie Wilder, Brackett was nominated for an Academy Award for his adaptation of *Ninotchka* (1939) [they probably would have won had it not been for another little movie called *Gone With the Wind*]. Some of his other works include: *Hold back the Dawn* (1941); *Lost Weekend* (1945), *A Foreign Affair* (1948). In the 1950 he experimented with science fiction with *Journey to the Center of the Earth* (1959). He also wrote *Niagara* (1953) which would star Marilyn Monroe.

The 1955 movie, *The Girl on the Red Velvet Swing*, was written and produced by Brackett. The story is based on the true story of Evelyn Nesbit Thaw and Sanford White. White was shot by Evelyn's slightly deranged husband Harry Thaw. White, an architect by training, is credited with designing one of the "Cottages" on Clinton Street. The Thaw/White story, although not occurring in Saratoga, has always been associated with the city because of the house on Clinton. Charles would have heard the story as a youth. It is somehow fitting that a story with a Saratoga connection would be one of Brackett's last films.

By his first wife, Elizabeth Fletcher, Charles had two daughters. When Elizabeth died in 1943, Charles married Lillian "Buff" Fletcher who lived until 1984. The women were sisters. His daughter, Alexandra Brackett Larmore, lived in Hollywood while his daughter, Mrs. Clifford Moore, lived in Washington D.C.

BROADWAY

614

Lawrence

The house at 614 appeared destined to the same lonely fate as the house at 604; however, when this house's luck changed it changed dramatically. In 1899, Franklin Lawrence and his family moved into the house; a residence they would maintain for the next 35 years.

In the 1880s this house experienced significant turnover and for several years it even stood empty. It was rented as a seasonal cottage by Silas Briggs, an attorney in New York City (his daughter married Augustine Shepherd (25 Gr). He was followed by William Stone Smith, a Troy steel manufacturer, who would rent this house for three seasons. Eventually, Smith would build his own house at 655 Broadway. The final seasonal tenant was Franklin Gale also of Troy.

When Lawrence first moved into the house he listed his occupation as manager of the Excelsior Spring. The Excelsior is off the beaten path in the valley northeast of the village. Because of its location, the spring's economic usefulness was from bottling the water more than as a spring people visited when they were out for a stroll.

Lawrence eventually purchased the Excelsior Spring and expanded his operation to include the Quivic Spring. He built a bottling plant, parts of which still remain on Excelsior Springs Avenue. One of his wisest decisions was when he began bottling water under the name Quivic Vichy. It soon became a very popular drink. Lawrence continued to diversify his operation, opening a printing plant at the same site.

The McNair Family

Antoine de Reilhe McNair Jr. was from one of the oldest and most sustained military families in America. For over fifty years, McNair and his family lived in a house that stood at the corner of Broadway and Rock Street. The McNair home has been replaced by a church. McNair moved into the house after his early retirement from the navy in 1872 and stayed until shortly before his death in 1923. McNair, like many other people who lived on North Broadway, adopted Saratoga as his home.

The record of the McNair family's military service on behalf of this country begins with Lieutenant David McNair, who served in the Continental Army under George Washington. At the outbreak of the Revolutionary War, the McNair family was living on a farm outside Philadelphia. Lieutenant David McNair took part in famous Christmas day crossing of the Delaware River and subsequent Battle of Trenton in December of 1776. David would die a month and half later as the result of wounds and exposure he received at the Battle of Princeton.

David's eldest son and fifth child, Alexander, was born in 1775. In 1794, nineteen year-old Alexander served in the county militia. When President Washington called up the militias to put down the Whiskey Rebellion, Alexander was one of those who served.

One of the first challenges to the authority of our new country was the Whiskey Rebellion which erupted in Western Pennsylvania in 1794. The issue was the perception among the residents of the western parts of most of the first states (mostly rural) that they were not defended by the wealthier eastern regions. In Pennsylvania the issue became the lack of support by the government in the eastern part of the state for insurrections involving the Native Americans. When told they owed a tax on the whiskey they produced, residents in the western counties refused to pay holding that they did not owe an authority that did not defend them. The rebellion was put down by force of arms; Alexander, being part of the force that quelled the minor rebellion.

Alexander was also involved in several Indian insurrections. His service resulted in his rising to the rank of Lieutenant of the infantry, a distinction. His promotion was granted to him by President Washington.

At thirty Alexander moved from Pennsylvania to Missouri which had been purchased only the year before; he was present for the transfer of title in March 1804. The reason Alexander left Pennsylvania is an interesting example of a mother's tough love. Alexander's father, David, died without a will. Alexander's mother, a woman who apparently valued strength, said that the farm would go to whichever son won a wrestling match. Alexander lost to a younger brother and Missouri won a true leader.

Alexander held several public offices in Missouri including sheriff. When the war of 1812 broke out, Alexander served as the colonel in a militia unit referred to as the Missouri Rangers; a cavalry troop. Following the war, Alexander continued to hold public offices including Marshal and Register of Deeds. When Missouri became a state in 1820, Alexander was elected as the first Governor defeating William Clark, the famous explorer who had served as territorial governor for the previous seven years. Alexander was only governor for one term.

A successful businessman, Alexander organized the American Fur Company which was in competition with the Hudson Bay Company. Alexander was also the Indian commissioner. He died in 1825 of influenza he caught while at one of the Indian camps.

Alexander married Margaret Susanne de Reilhe, whose royalist family had fled France for New Orleans during the French Revolution. Alexander and Margaret had twelve children. Their first son, Antoine de Reilhe McNair Sr., was named in honor of his mother's family. Antoine was a lieutenant in the Blackhawk War where he was crippled by a wound he received during one of the battles. Two of Alexander's other sons died in the Mexican War.

Antoine married three times. His second wife was Elvina Johnson of New Orleans. The couple had a set of twins but only one, Antoine Jr, lived. This is the first member of the family to live on Broadway in Saratoga.

Antoine Jr. was raised in New Orleans and Missouri. In 1856 Antoine was given an appointment to Naval Academy. He graduated in 1860 and served the Civil War on a series of ships. He was engaged in the battle of Savannah and numerous other battles receiving a wound in the capture of the Morris Island Batteries. After the war, while most officers were being demoted, Antoine was promoted to lieutenant-commander. He would serve in the West Indies and as inspector at Norfolk, VA. For one year he was a professor at the Naval Academy. He retired in 1872 as result of injuries he had received in 1868; coincidently, this was the same year his father died and he inherited a significant fortune.

Antoine moved to Saratoga where he married Frances Clarke, daughter of Benedict Clarke a successful person in his own right. The couple had three children: a son Frederic; daughter Frances; their second son, Alec, died of meningitis at age 5.

While he was in Saratoga, Antoine was very active serving for fifteen years on the board of education, and as the treasure of the United States Toboggan, the organization that operated the run at the Glen Mitchell. He was also secretary and treasurer of the bicycle club, and treasurer of the Athenaeum. Since he did not work and did not hold any position while living in Saratoga, he listed his occupation as "own investments."

The family's military service continued with Antoine's only surviving son, Frederick P. McNair. Born in Saratoga in 1873, Frederick was educated in the public high school, graduating as president of the class of 1892. Frederick received an appointment to the Military Academy at West Point. Unfortunately, he had to resign after two years (1894) because of frequent attacks of tonsillitis. Disappointed, Frederick returned to Saratoga where he began the study of law first with Judge Houghton (601 Br), then with A. W. Shepherd (27 Gr). Before he finished his law studies Frederick used family connections to secure a lucrative position in St Louis, Missouri. In 1898 Frederick left for the Midwest. Within months the Spanish American War broke out and Frederick returned to Saratoga so that he could enlist in the local militia. He entered the service as a private, serving with his fellow Saratogians at a series of forts in the south. In September 1898 he was commissioned a lieutenant. Almost immediately he was stricken with malaria and died October 18, 1898. His epitaph in Greenridge Cemetery tells much of this family's philosophy; it reads "He did his duty."

In 1899, a book was published with brief biographies of people from Saratoga County. Antoine used an entry in the book to serve as the epitaph for his only son, the legacy, and pride of his life. For a reader who would like to experience the tribute of a father for his lost son, this is must read.

The American legacy of the military McNairs would seem to have come to an end with the passing of Frederick and the end of the male line. Frederick's sister, Frances, would have liked that to have been true. Unfortunately, the military tradition had one leg left. Frederick's sibling, Frances, married into the Mather family of Albany. She had three children, only one of whom she gave the family name. That son was Alexander McNair Mather in honor of her of her great-grandfather, the Governor of Missouri. Alexander died in Holland during the Second World War; the legacy was finally over.

Despite their relative wealth and prominence, the McNair family shares a humble burial plot with their in-laws, the Clarks. It is at the crest of the eastern-most hill in Greenridge Cemetery. The McNairs rest with others of local status; the Davisons (417 Br); the McEwens (1 FS); and Does (505 Br); all of whom did much for the community but are all but forgotten today.

Riggi Palazzo

Imagine for a minute that you were in a position to build the house of your dreams; a house that suited you, your family and your lifestyle. Building such a house might be everyone's dream; occasionally a person's opportunity; but Michele and Ron Riggi, who actually took on the task, learned that it was also a time consuming responsibility.

The question one would have upon seeing anyone's completed project is, when they set out to build the house what were they trying to create? Michele does not even hesitate as she responds, "A home for my family; a place that represents us and what we value."

One of the city's brochures refers to the house's style as French Chateauesque. That is not the term Michele would use feeling instead that the house is a blend of styles some French, more Italian, but ultimately all Riggi.

There was never a question about whether their house would be in Saratoga; it had to be. Although neither Ron nor Michele had grown up in the city, both were from the area and knew Saratoga and what it offered. Michele's feelings, that Saratoga is a beautiful, quaint and safe place to live, are shared by so many of those who reside in the city. Michele added, "It is a great place to bring up children." The tone of her voice demonstrated the pride she has in her adopted city.

Perhaps the best measure that this house is a home was in Michele's response to the time old question; how many bedrooms are there? "Just enough for my family." The simple fact is that this magnificent house was built to be a family home. It may be a showpiece in the community but it is first and foremost a home for the Riggis.

The Riggis have adopted a philosophy that goes back to Saratoga's roots; guests are encouraged to stay in the local hotels. This is not done to be cold but rather to avoid the stress that is brought on by living in close proximity with less familiar people.

The choice of stone

Stone houses are permanent; they exude strength, stability, and a sense of permanence; all images Michele had for her dream house. To her there was no question the house had to be made out of stone.

Michele would soon learn that it is in the construction that stone creates the biggest problems. This is a country where few houses use stone in their construction; and what stone is used is almost always just a facade. The first issue was finding workers who could build a house of this magnitude *made* of stone, not just accented by it. The answer was international craftsmen.

There was a reason why the house took three to four years to build. The time was required for the craftsmen and artists to address all the intricate details. Every stone in the house had to be beveled and each element had to be custom built which meant additional time (each stone had to be hand cut). Unlike a brick building which has even rows, the stones in the Riggi home are all different sizes making the walls a complex puzzle. The fine points are everywhere; from the mantels over the windows and fireplaces; to the fencing, verandas, pools, and even the garages; care was given as to how each feature would appear.

Another issue was how to take something as strong and potentially cold as stone and make it look and feel warm. The solution lay in two very different decisions; the design of the house and the setting. The house was built only two stories tall avoiding the appearance of a castle that a taller building may have given. The numerous widows take away the potential appearance of a fortress.

Since a building's amiability is also controlled by its environment; suitable landscaping was key to adding warmth. The entire area surrounding the house is broken up into a collection of independent venues; pools, fountains, lawns, formal gardens, verandas, an area for the dogs, an outdoor pavilion. Visitors are guided through the various gardens and lawns by walkways made of light colored stone, edged with darker stone.

The house is as strong and unique inside as it is out. The stone of the outside continues into the house with all eleven bathrooms made completely of marble. The outside is also continued in the foyer with a fresco that suggests to a visitor that they are in a Roman square.

Themes

There is no wallpaper; instead, the walls have frescoes. To achieve the look she wanted fifteen artists from around the world were brought in. While Michele chose the textures, fabrics and furniture for each room, the artists were busy creating original artwork. The artists selected were so talented that in the foyer one can not tell when standing two feet away that what appears to be marble is really frescoed.

Michele describes the overall theme of the lower level floor as "safari;" after visiting the house and seeing the blend of Asian, African and Italian pieces, the term "sophisticated international" seems equally appropriate.

One of the most delicate balances that has been reached is in having the rooms larger than in a typical house, yet still small enough to be intimate. In large part this is because the house is broken up into numerous rooms rather than large open spaces.

There is extensive red velvet fabrics with leopard and cheetah prints used in the theater, while other rooms are accented in zebra and elephant. Each room in the house has its own theme. The themes vary but are matched to the room's function. The theater –yes there is a theater – probably best exemplifies the blend. Down to such details as the stage, the room is designed to look like a scaled-down model of the Paris Opera House in the movie *Moulin Rouge*. The theater seats twelve and is outfitted with a candy counter which only carries treats in the same size boxes one buys at the movies.

The house has an element not immediately visible from the sidewalk. The ground around the front of the lower level was excavated to allow full size windows that are technically below ground level. This feature allows the gym to be immersed in natural light.

To keep their four grown children wanting to visit each of their bedrooms is its own living space. The spaces, which include individual verandas, are different but similar to suites, not studio apartments. The four bedrooms are themed around how Michele sees that child:

- The oldest daughter's room is done in English Dorchester. Both the bedroom and the adjacent terrace emanate grace, strength and a sense of feminine strength.

- The younger daughter, who is artistic, has a room done in furnishings from India and Pakistan. The slope of the ceiling and metal frame over the bed provide the feeling of being in an elegant birdcage.
- One son is the historian. It was only natural that his room would be done in parchment. The dark walls and ceiling are covered in hand drawn maps.
- The younger son is interested in acting and loves activities involving water from swimming to waterskiing. His room is done in an underwater theme.

Michele chose all the decorations. The children did not object, knowing that the final product would be successful.

Asked if there was any part of the house that she would describe as turning out exactly the way it was envisioned, Michele did not hesitate when she responded: "All of it. I was involved in every aspect of the house from the initial planning, through the years of construction, to the selection of each piece of furniture. The entire house turned out the way it was imagined."

Anyone who has ever been involved in the design and building of his or her own house has some regret when it is completed. Not so for Michele. She enjoys entertaining and wishes that the dining room was bigger. Since the lot is triangular it was not large enough to allow the dimensions desired for the dining room. The reason she was not disappointed is that she knew of the restriction before ground was broken.

When the interview was over and the article was being written it became apparent that the most important question had not been asked. "Was it worth it?" The first reaction was frustration at the error, then the reason the question was missed became obvious. Anyone who discusses the house with Michele soon realizes that she loves Riggi Palazzo. She may wish it had been completed sooner, and that the problems one always has building a house had not occurred, but the simple fact is her love of her house was worth whatever the obstacles.

Author's comment:

Whether to include this house created a dilemma. The self imposed restriction that to be in the book a house should be built prior to 1920 would have kept this house out. This house was significantly newer but has a very marked presence in Saratoga. To ignore the house made no sense and as an historian I wondered what a reader would think a hundred years from now about its omission.

Expecting no response I contacted the owners and offered three options: a picture with virtually no commentary; a commentary on the house; or a commentary on the family similar to the stories about the other homes on the street. I should not have been surprised when the Riggis proved to be like virtually everyone else I have met in my investigation, proud of their home and wanting its story told.

Since they were the builder and still living in the house it was hard to think historically. The only way to write the story of the palazzo was to treat it like a magazine article.

An historian a hundred years from now can write of the family.
Hollis

BROADWAY

626

Hamilton

Theodore Hamilton was a man who was blessed with an interesting, if short, life. Born in 1851 in Rochester, New York, Hamilton attended the public schools while he lived in his native city.

Theodore Hamilton's father, for whom he was named, was a lawyer. The senior Hamilton died in 1863 as a result of an illness he contracted while serving in the cavalry during the Civil War. Following his father's death, Hamilton's mother moved to New York City.

Without his father's income, twelve year-old Hamilton went to work for a commercial business days and attended high school in the evening. After graduation he was given a position as a reporter for the *New York Sun*. His biggest story was when he covered the murder of railroad financier James Fisk Jr. by Edward Stokes, an unusual account for such a young reporter. While at the *Sun*, Hamilton started reading for the law and attending lectures at Columbia University. In 1872 at the age of 21, Hamilton was admitted to the bar (he had already worked full time for nine years).

Shortly after his admission to the bar, Hamilton moved to Ballston Spa where he set up his own law practice. He remained in Ballston Spa until 1886 when he was elected District Attorney. That year he moved to this house on North Broadway. He would reelected District Attorney. While in Ballston Spa, Hamilton married Kate Luther; they had three daughters, Margaret, Mary, Kathryn and one son, Macaulay (called Thomas). Hamilton demonstrated his interest in history by naming his son after Thomas Babington Macaulay, the English essayist.

There were two trials for which Hamilton is most noted. The first was the trial of Arthur McQuade, a New York City alderman.

McQuade was charged with accepting a kickback from a railroad company to facilitate its obtaining a franchise. The trial was moved to Saratoga County from New York City in an effort to obtain an unbiased jury. As county district attorney, Hamilton served as the third prosecutor (the first two were from New York City). The defense was led by Jesse L'Amoreaux of Ballston, joined by John Foley (34 Cr) and James Houghton (601 Br). McQuade was not foolish and knew the advantage using local attorneys would have on the jury – he was acquitted.

The second trial followed a few months after McQuade. It was the murder trial of Robinski, who was convicted and sentenced to life in prison.

In his later life Hamilton's major clients were the railroads. In addition to his primary client the Fitchburg Railroad, Hamilton also represented the Boston & Maine RR and the Troy Terminal RR. Hamilton was the president of Saratoga Traction Company (STC). The STC was an above ground electric railroad that had service out to the lake and out to the Geysers (later the line was extended to Ballston Spa).

Hamilton also edited and published a book on legal negligence cases - he was considered an expert.

He was one of the trustees on the Saratoga Athenaeum and School of Design, a subscription library. The names of the other trustees, most of which appear in the index, show the prestige that the institution held. He was also on the board of trustees for the Hawley Home for Children.

In December of 1904, Hamilton hurried home from a meeting in New York City to meet with a client in his home office. When the client arrived Hamilton shook hands and sat back down behind his desk. Suddenly, he slumped over in his chair. He had died almost instantly of a heart attack. He was 53.

Hamilton's uncle, Dr. Frank Hamilton, was called in as a consultant after Garfield was shot.

BROADWAY

630

Wheeler

"He died nobly; and perhaps only a day before us. I want no nobler record with which to end my life, than his coolness, bravery and manliness." These were the words of Col. Winsor French (718 Br)when he wrote to the people of Saratoga to announce the death of Luther Wheeler, one of the village's favorite sons. The community's respect for young Wheeler was so deep that the American Legion Post is named in his honor.

Captain Luther Wheeler was killed in the Battle of Mayre's Heights. The battle happened in early May of 1863, two months before Gettysburg. There were two reasons why the news of Wheeler's death had a devastating yet unifying impact on the village. Wheeler had enlisted as a lieutenant and his skills and leadership had earned him the rank of captain when he was only 23. What made his Civil War death even more notable was that Wheeler had predicted when it would happen. Before the battle he told his troops that if they crossed the stream he would die. He was shot less than one hundred yards from the creek.

It is said that the only time the men saw Col. French have tears in his eyes during the entire war was when he was informed of Captain Wheeler's death.

Luther died too young to have his own house but this was the home of his brother, Frank. Until his death, Frank was a school principal who resigned to become a ticket agent. After Frank's death, his wife operated an upscale boarding house in what had been the family home.

Frank was a member of first baseball team, a village trustee and a Mason.

BROADWAY

634

Rickard

There are people who are attracted to the act of sales; what they sell is of lesser importance. Sydney Rickard was one of those who knew and loved sales.

For almost twenty years from 1868 through 1886, Rickard was a successful merchant on Broadway. His store sold decorating materials with merchandise that included wallpaper, shades, frames, draperies and artist materials. It was the right store at the right time as this was a period of home improvements and hotel expansions in Saratoga. Families throughout the village were installing kitchens, bathrooms, and in some cases even central heat. People of all classes were using wallpaper to cover up marks in their rough plastered walls, and adding drapes. In home decorations there was always the sure business of wooden houses needing to be painted every few years. Starting from almost nothing, Rickard's business was profitable enough that he was able to build this house. Rickard loved horses and built this house with a stable suitable to hold his span of chestnuts and bay.

In the 1880s Rickard had a store had that served a local clientele. By the mid 1890s he was selling pharmaceuticals throughout North America. The reason for the change was that he was fortunate to be one of the early investors in G. F. Harvey Company. By the mid-1890s he was the vice-president of the company, and later he was the president. Much of the success that the company enjoyed is attributed to Rickard's administrative skills.

Rickard and his wife, Minerva, had a somewhat atypical marriage. She was six years older (unusual at the time). She was strong willed serving as one of the founders of the Saratoga Hospital and working for the Home of the Good Shepherd. Later she was listed as being one of the managers of the Hospital. The couple had two sons; one died when he was five, the other, when he was still a young man. He did live long enough to marry.

Rickard was forced to work long hours trying to get G. F. Harvey Co. started. Eventually the stress became too much and his health failed him. He retired for health reasons about the time he turned fifty. In an effort to regain his vigor, Rickard and his wife toured Europe. When he returned he was believed to be better but his health again failed in the spring of 1902. That August, as the season in Saratoga was drawing to a close, he died; he was 54. Minerva would continue her philanthropic efforts until her death in 1924.

Rickard was too busy running his businesses to be involved in politics. He was involved with his community serving as one of the directors and officers of the YMCA, which benefited extensively from his social benevolence. It was, however, the Congregational Church on Circular Street (now condominiums) that was the major recipient of his philanthropic support. In the memory of his son he donated much of the money necessary to build the edifice.

NO. CIRCULAR

2

Woolley

Which came first: the man, the role, or the trademark beard? More importantly, does it matter if you have a Star on the Hollywood Walk of Fame and were nominated for two Academy Awards?

Those who knew Actor Monty Woolley as an older man have described him as a cross between the characters he played in his two most famous roles; that of Sheridan Whiteside in *The Man Who Came to Dinner* and the role of Madden Thomas in *Life Begins at 8:30*. These descriptions are hardly complimentary as Sheridan is a crotchety curmudgeon who inflicted himself on others and Madden is an old actor who has allowed years of alcohol abuse to bring him down and has trouble accepting how his life ultimately turned out.

Known today for his famous Van Dyke beard, Woolley was nominated for two Academy Awards. The parts for which he was nominated were Best Actor in the Leading Role for Howard in *The Pied Piper* (1943); and Best Actor in a Supporting Role for playing Colonel William G. Smollett in *Since You Went Away* (1945). He was not nominated for the roles that seemed to suit him best; Whiteside, or the one time he actually played himself in Cole Porter's *Night and Day* (1946).

Born in New York City, Woolley came to Saratoga when his father became the proprietor of the Grand Union Hotel. His father also operated the Bristol Hotel in Manhattan. The two residences allowed young Monty the opportunity to meet some of the leading people in the theater at the time.

After attending a private boarding school Woolley entered Yale University in 1907. Two years later he would meet a fellow student known for his musical talent, Cole Porter. Their friendship would extend through their entire life. As time went on, it became more evident that Porter enjoyed the company of men. Although Woolley never married and frequently socialized with Porter, their names were not associated in intimate terms. It appears everyone accepted their friendship.

A director before he was an actor, Woolley would direct three of Porter's musicals; *Fifty Million Frenchmen*; *Little Show* and *Jubilee*.

In the 1950s Woolley did several live television spots. It was an inappropriate venue for a stage actor. New York Times quoted his impression of what it was like appearing on television saying, "I was nervous and watched the clock constantly. I thought it was all terrible."

Woolley was known for his arrogance, excellent memory and ability to spend each evening that he was in town sharing conversation over a beer with one of Saratoga's other true characters, Frank Sullivan.

Woolley died in May 1963. The cause of death was a combination of kidney and heart ailments. His estate was estimated to be over $350,000. His maid received $35,000; his alma mater, Yale, received his collection of original Shakespearean plays; and the local library was bequeathed the remainder of his book collection.

Two Saratoga natives and childhood associates collaborated on one movie. Woolley played Prof. Wutheridge in the movie *The Bishop's Wife* which was written by Charles Brackett (605 Br).

The Woolley family lived several places in Saratoga. While his father was active in the Grand Union Hotel, the family lived in the hotel claiming their address at 28 Washington; one of the cottages. Later they would move to 3 Clement and after that to the French House (718 Br).

BROADWAY

649

Brown

There are careers that have changed appreciably making them more or less appealing than today. There are also positions that at one time had appreciably more influence.

Orton Brown started as the room clerk at the Union (Grand Union) Hotel. The role of room clerk has changed dramatically since Orton's service. Unlike today, where there are few differences in the rooms within a given hotel, a hundred fifty years ago every room was different.

Under the American Plan everyone in the hotel may have to eat the same foods but the differences in rooms made their assignment a very personal decision. When Orton was room clerk it was nearly impossible to please all the guests. Everyone wanted rooms facing the quiet garden, not on the noisy street (without air conditioning widows were left open). No one wanted to be near the rattling elevator and every guest wanted to be at the end of the hall. While one season two families might want to near each other so their children might associate, the next season one of the families might want their daughter far away from the other couple's son; to complicate the issue neither family would want to be reassigned. To further confuse the issues there were guests who would stay the whole season and others staying only one night. The pressures on the room clerk were incredible and Orton earned the money he used for this house.

We can be sure Orton was good at his position. When the United States reopened in 1874 Orton changed hotels. Commodore Vanderbilt changed with him "because of his friendship" with Orton.

Orton married twice but had no children that survived. His second wife, who he married when they were both much older, was Allena Butler (596 Br).

BROADWAY

655

Smith

William Stone Smith was born and educated in New York City. He moved to Troy in 1865 when he was 24 years old.

Creating a steel company named Burnett and Smith, William became reasonably wealthy. He married his partner's daughter, Frances, who died without having children. When his father-in-law died, William remained in a partnership this time with his brother-in-law. The name of the company did not change, although it did incorporate.

He would later marry Alice Bontecou Cross with whom he had one daughter, Mary. The second Mrs. Smith, William, and Mary made a practice of spending the season in Saratoga. For several years they rented 614 Broadway, the house at the corner of Rock.

Realizing that they both enjoyed summers in Saratoga, in about 1897 they had this house built. Before 1906 the house had become the family's primary residence. William became an early commuter taking a train to Troy each day. Even with the move he would retain his directorships on two banks; Central National Bank, and the National City Bank both were in Troy. He also owned stock in the Adirondack Trust Company.

When he was a young man, Smith loved sculling, a very popular pastime. Later he took up yachting, owning several boats.

On November 13, 1906, Smith took an early train home. By 7:00 that evening he experienced an embolism and died almost immediately. He was 65. His widow would retain the home for several years.

BROADWAY

658

Wayland
Mansion

Thrice married; thrice widowed; but very wealthy.

There are times when one clue opens the door to an interesting story. That was the case when it was learned that in the 1880s this house was known as the Wayland Mansion.

The Wayland family is among the oldest in Saratoga. The First Wayland was Reverend Frances Wayland who immigrated from England. He was a minister at the First Baptist Church in Saratoga who somehow accumulated a small fortune. Two of his daughters would operate a girls' school on Broadway. His son Frances attended Union College eventually earned his doctorate and became the President of Brown University in Providence, R.I.

As compelling as the Wayland family was it is, however, his daughter-in-law and one of the last with the family name to live in the house that is the more interesting character. Mary Young was the daughter of Col. Samuel Young, one of the leading statesmen and politicians of the area. Young earned his military title in 1814 when, while also serving in the state assembly, was appointed as a military aide. He was twice speaker of the state legislature, a county judge, Secretary of State for the state, nominated for governor and served in the state senate. Young and his wife Mary Gibson, had a daughter Mary born in 1818. Mary would become known for her beauty, grace, manors and her repeated widowhood.

In 1838, Mary married John Beach, son of Miles Beach a wealthy businessman and the postmaster of Saratoga. John and Mary would have one child, a daughter, also named Mary born in 1844. John's older brother William A. Beach was one of the most famous lawyers in the country. Perhaps it was because he was tired of living near such a notorious brother, or perhaps it was his desire for adventure but in 1849, John joined the gold rush leaving Saratoga for California. John would die in 1850 while in California. The same year Mary's father, Samuel Young, died. For five years Mary stayed near her husband's family in Saratoga. The story of the Beach family will be given in a future volume.

In 1855, Mary married for a second time. This marriage was to a character named Col. Charles Burr, the son of a wealthy businessman. At the time of Charles' father's death in 1844, Burr was living an interesting life. Burr was living off the pittance he could earn peddling books and staying and eating with friends in Albany. Charles' lifestyle was in part the result of his father having banished him from the family's house. Fortunately his father had never gotten around to officially disinheriting his only son. Burr's extended family was sure that they were going to inherit the elder Burr's estate and were shocked when it was learned that he died without a will.

Charles Burr went from living in the unheated backrooms of acquaintances to being wealthy overnight. To prevent him wasting his money Charles' extended family sought to have him declared insane. He did not fight the claim instead accepting that his money would be administered by one lawyer and a second lawyer would be sure he had what he needed.

Three years later, 1847, Charles Burr snapped out of whatever was bothering him and he sued for control of his own money and won. As one would expect of someone with his problems, Burr attracted a group of people all too willing to live on whatever crumbs he would cast their way.

Suddenly in 1855, Burr was all the news when it was learned that he planned to marry the beautiful widow Mary Young Beach. That is when he disappeared. It was claimed that he was tricked by his associates into leaving town temporarily, thus avoiding the wedding. His departure may have been his own idea but whatever the reasons Burr was suddenly missing. An article reporting the situation appeared in the *New York Times* and Burr came forward saying he did not know anyone was looking for him.

The marriage occurred in late July 1855 but not before Charles signed over half his fortune to Mary. The couple, along with her daughter by her first marriage would live in Saratoga until Charles' death in 1860.

Following commencement in 1855, Frances Wayland D.D. retired after 28 years as President of Brown University. He wanted time to write and study. He moved back to Saratoga, his birthplace, where five years later he married Mary Young Beach Burr. She was 42 he was almost 65. Frances Wayland was a published author and a man of some respect. He would die in October of 1865 leaving Mary a 47 year-old widow for the third time.

Mary would live in the house for almost two decades. Finally her daughter Mary Beach would marry John Ehninger an artist and illustrator. He was the man who designed the symbol for the city still in use. Mary and John would live in a house on the corner of Broadway and Greenfield. In her later years Mary Wayland would move in with her daughter. The Wayland Mansion would be rented.

The house would have a series of notable residents including state senators, coal dealers, and bankers.

BROADWAY

659

Cluett

Over the course of his connection with Saratoga, George B. Cluett rented several houses before having two constructed for his family. This Colonial Revival is the second of the houses he had built, the first being on Clement Street. Since this is his later house, this section will talk about his life between 1895, the year of the first house, until his death in 1912. The discussion about his earlier success will be covered in the section on the house on Clement Street.

In 1905 when this house was finished, George B. Cluett had been retired for two years from the day-to-day operations of his factories. In retirement Cluett continued as the director of several charitable organizations in Troy and served on the board of directors of two banks.

The previous decade he had been acknowledged as the principal partner in Cluett, Peabody and Company, the largest collar, cuff and shirt manufacturing operation in this country and perhaps the world. The company Cluett formed would change its name several times before it eventually became part of the Arrow Shirt Company. At the time of Cluett's retirement the company's operations in Troy had expanded until the main factory was four hundred feet long, one hundred feet deep and six stories tall. There were over 1,000 operators at this one site with other smaller factories in the region and around the country. Additionally, the company had people doing piece work out of their homes. At one point Cluett Peabody had over 4,000 employees. At the turn of the last century anything that happened to the Cluett operations had an economic impact on the entire area.

While he worked, Cluett's supervisory responsibilities necessitated that he be near his factories, so he resided primarily in Troy. In retirement Cluett developed a new pattern for residences. He would winter in Palm Beach, Florida; spend a few weeks in the spring in Troy before coming to his summer residence in Saratoga. When he left Saratoga in the fall he would return to Troy for a few weeks, then on to his winter home in Palm Beach.

When this house was built Cluett had already been seriously ill, which was the reason for his retirement. Known from his earliest days for his generosity to worthwhile causes, it was almost natural that retirement and illness would shift his focus from the accumulation of worth to providing for humanitarian needs.

All three of the communities, where Cluett had homes, benefited from the family's active social and philanthropic role. Cluett's contributions in Saratoga to such organizations as the libraries of the YMCA and Hawley Home (the village's orphanage on Ludlow), and his contribution to the hospital were dwarfed by his contributions in Troy and internationally. In Troy he was one of the primary contributors to the newly created Samaritan Hospital; he would remain a member on its board of directors until his death. He was a major contributor to the Troy YMCA, YWCA, and founded a boys club in his adopted city. In memory of their father, George and his brother J. W. R. (see 3 Cl) provided the Methodist Church in Troy with a spire (neither brother attended that church but their father did). He also provided churches with organs and the private school where one of his son's had attended he gave a new gymnasium.

One evening Cluett attended a lecture by a missionary serving in Labrador. In addition to discussing the region and the issues of the indigenous people of the area, the missionary used the opportunity to try to raise financial aid. The missionary told the audience that the mission was using one old, inadequate ship to serve numerous communities along the desolate windswept shore. The mission's needs or accomplishments somehow touched Cluett emotionally and he ordered that a schooner with a back-up auxiliary engine be constructed. Not only was the ship capable of carrying essential supplies, it was constructed with a small clinic. The mission named the ship the *George B. Cluett* in honor of its donor. It was noted in the newspapers that when one of Cluett's daughters christened the ship, she used a bottle of spring water rather than the customary Champaign.

Almost exactly as the ship was completed and fitted out, a freak storm hit Labrador and destroyed the original ship of the mission. The new vessel, the *George B. Cluett*, was supplied and dispatched to aid the communities along the coast. The tale of the ship leaving in a fog bank to serve the needs of those who had lost their access to the outside world was reported extensively in the *New York Times*. It was a tale similar to those involved in the rescues in Hurricane Katrina in 2005.

George B. Cluett died June 29, 1912. A British immigrant who had started with little, Cluett left an estate worth over five million dollars. At the time it was the largest estate ever filed in Rensselaer County.

***

Cluett's youngest son, Alfonso, would die as a young man. The Pawling School for Boys was built in his memory.

George B. Cluett's son, E. Harold Cluett, would be the company treasurer, vice president and chairman of the board. He would serve for six years as the congressmen from Troy.

Cluett's nephew, Sanford Cluett, would develop a process that would reduce the effect shrinking would have on the shape of a shirt. The process would be licensed as Sanforized.

BROADWAY

687

Ludlow

This home was built from the income made on the patent and manufacturing of primarily one item. The item is the answer to this riddle: What is something you see every day and never notice; hope is near your house and never used?

In the early 1840s Henry Ludlow graduated from Union College's engineering program. It was a time when industries and communities were growing. Where wells once served the fresh water needs of the residents, suddenly there was a demand for city wide water systems. Communities throughout the country were building reservoirs and laying underground pipes to support a comprehensive water system to meet the expanding demand. At the same time most buildings, if not completely made of wood, were wood framed. Fires were a constant threat.

Ludlow was the right man with the right idea at the right time patenting and manufacturing fire hydrants. A fire hydrant is really just a gigantic high pressure valves. The Ludlow Valves Company also manufactured gas, water, steam, and oil valves.

Ludlow Valves Company was founded in 1866. The company was originally located in Waterford; however, by 1872 it was expanding and required more space so it moved to Lansingburg. In the 1890s Ludlow Valves again relocated, this time to south Troy. The last move was at about the same time that Ludlow sold his interest in the company.

The Ludlow Valves Company followed the same cycle as many manufacturing industries that started out in the northeast. It grew and prospered until the end of World War II. To remain competitive, in the 1960, Ludlow Valves merged with Rensselaer Valves. By 1969 the company was closed with the rights sold to a southern manufacturer.

688

Green
Mansion

The names associated with this house from 1882 until 1905 reads like a cross between the list of hotel proprietors of Saratoga and the industrialists of Troy. During the period 1883 through 1889 the house was the residence of R. H. Southgate, who was the proprietor of three hotels; the Long Beach Hotel on Long Island: the Windsor hotel in Montreal and Congress Hall in Saratoga. For one year it was the residence of Charles Brown from New York City who, along with his wife, hosted two parties that season worthy of note in the *New York Times*. From 1890 through 1893 the house was the residence of James Breslin who, in conjunction with two partners, operated the Grand Union Hotel.

The house was rented to three Trojans starting with the Ludlow family before they built their own home at 687 Broadway. Charles Cleminshaw rented for one year before the house was the residence of Frank Gilbert of Mohawk and Hudson Paper Company. Gilbert's company is still in existence today in Cohoes. For two seasons Sali Stark, a merchant from New York City, occupied the cottage. He was followed by Robert Cluett of the Cluett family in Troy.

After two more seasons the house was finally purchased and made the seasonal residence of Col. Edward M. Green. The house eventually became the year around residence for the Green family from whom it receives its name. When he moved to Saratoga, Green was older and only commuted to Troy when necessary.

Edward Green was a direct descendant of Nathan Green one of the heroes of the Revolutionary War. Edward's father, Hannibal, started a wholesale steel business in Troy in 1809. Edward expanded the operation to include Troy Bridge Company. He was still operating the companies when he died in 1923 at the age of 77.

Too young to serve in the Civil War, Green enlisted in the militia in the late 1860s eventually earning the rank of Colonel. A title he used throughout his life even though he was never called upon for active service. Physically active Green was the chief of the Arba Read Steam Fire Engine Company in Troy; a volunteer company.

Edward Green joined numerous clubs including the Troy Club, Union League of New York City, and the Saratoga Club. An avid golfer, Green was not only a member of the Saratoga Golf Club and McGregor Links but also at different times, the president of both clubs.

Green's philanthropic activities focused on the needs of orphans; however, he did provide for the relatively new humane society.

The house required a large staff. According to the 1910 census there were seven servants. They were as follows; one butler, one coachman; one footman; one cook; one waitress; two maids.

His widow, Elizabeth Harte Green, and their son Griswald would live in the Saratoga house until her death in 1931, a total of 28 years. After Elizabeth's death the house stood empty for two years (it was the height of the depression). Eventually it was occupied by two widows both named Shutts.

(BROADWAY)

695

Drexel
Mansion

In examining the history of the Drexel family it would appear that the youngest son, Joseph, who was authoritative enough in his own business dealings, was controlled by his two older brothers in the family operations. His brothers' overpowering nature may explain why Joseph bought a cottage in Saratoga while their summer retreats were closer to the family's banking operations in Philadelphia. Having a strong-willed wife, four daughters and no sons may also explain why Joseph just wanted a place to get away.

The Drexel's considerable fortune originated with Joseph's Austrian father, Frances Drexel. As a young man, Frances was a portrait painter in which capacity he worked throughout Western Europe and South America. An artist, Frances instilled in his children an appreciation of art, culture and philanthropy that the family would adhere to for generations. Having traveled extensively fulfilling commissions, Frances developed an understanding of how currency values fluctuate and more importantly, how a wise investor could capitalize on the shifts. When he immigrated to America, Frances started a currency trading house in Philadelphia. A decade later Drexel & Company was one of the leading banks in the nation.

The Drexels, except for Joseph, were very private in both their social and business affairs. Discretion was necessary because they understood the effect that advance knowledge about where the family was considering investing would have on stock prices. Because of the family's secretive nature their influence in financing railroads, the Civil War, and several early businesses is often overlooked.

There were three Drexel brothers; Frances (named for his father), Anthony, and Joseph. Each of the brothers had a role in the bank. Although Anthony was second born, his innate business acronym resulted in his overseeing the family's banking operations. Frances, as oldest, was the titular head attending functions and serving as the face of the bank. Having Frances as the front person afforded Anthony the time necessary to supervise the operations and examine investments. Joseph was responsible for setting up the new branch banks in Chicago, New York City, London and Paris. In New York, Joseph and Anthony joined forces with an ambitious young man named J. Pierpont Morgan forming Drexel Morgan Bank. In 1876, at the age of 43, Joseph Drexel retired from the bank. For the remainder of his short life, Joseph devoted himself to philanthropy and the arts.

Under Anthony's guidance, the Drexel bank was so successful that each brother's estate was valued in today's money as in excess of $100,000,000.

During Saratoga's post Civil War glory days; Joseph Drexel came each season bringing with him his four daughters and often being visited by his three nieces by his brother Frances and his seven nieces and nephews who were the children of his brother Anthony. Two of Joseph's own daughters, Miss Lucy and Miss Elizabeth, were regular visitors to the village even after their father passed. Lucy and Elizabeth married the brothers Eric and John Dahlgren respectively. Their husbands' father was an admiral in the Civil War and had amassed a fortune of his own.

While Saratoga's most famous hotels were built in the village, there were a few on the lake. Drexel made a bold move and built Balmoral, a four story hotel capable of hosting 300 guests on the top of Mt. McGregor. At this location guests were treated to a spectacular view, fresh air (the hotel was especially popular among those who suffered from seasonal hay fever) and entertainment. To facilitate the guests' trip from Saratoga to the hotel, Drexel and his partners built a ten mile long narrow gage railroad from Saratoga up to the top of the mountain. Perhaps because he had four daughters the Balmoral was the only hotel to feature a twelve piece orchestra made up exclusively of women musicians. The hotel was destroyed by fire in 1897.

The Drexel brothers were personal friends of General, later President Ulysses S. Grant. In 1885, Grant, who was dying from throat cancer, was trying to overcome some financial setbacks by writing his memoirs. The former President needed a quiet place to finish the text. In Saratoga, Joseph Drexel is probably best remembered for being the man who bought the former President a cottage on Mt. McGregor in which to write his memoirs. Although Grant only lived at the cottage for a few weeks, in the course of the next five years a quarter of a million people would ride the train up the mountain to visit the site of Grant's final moments. Drexel later gave the cottage to the State to set up a museum to honor the former President.

The Drexels were catholic and Joseph's wife, on her annual visit to Europe, frequently visited the Pope. One of her greatest prizes was a pair of fans given to her by Pope Leo X. It is said that the fans she gave him back were much more expensive; however, she cherished her pair because of their distinguished history.

Joseph's third daughter, Elizabeth, was the member of the family most attached to Saratoga. For that reason this section will focus on her life. In late June 1889 a little over a year after her father's death, Elizabeth married John Vinton Dahlgren. The ceremony was at St. Patrick's Cathedral in New York City, in what could only be described as pomp and grandeur. The church was decorated with potted palm trees brought in just for the wedding. Those attending the rite were so numerous that there were ten ushers including the son of the Secretary of State, the Spanish Vice Consul, and a French Count. The ceremony was presided over by the Archbishop of New York. The wedding was followed by a brunch at the Drexel's city residence at 103 Madison Avenue. For a wedding present John gave Elizabeth a family heirloom; the betrothal ring of Martin Luther to Catherine von Bora.

The marriage was considered somewhat audacious for a variety of reasons. It had only been a year since the patriarch's death; the minimal grieving time of the era. Although John was twenty-two he had just finished law school and had not yet set up a practice (it was not uncommon for lawyers not to marry until well into their thirties). Elizabeth was younger and hardly needed to rush into a marriage. To these potential miscues there was the fact that the groom's mother did not attend the wedding. To escape any scandal about the mother of the groom's possible displeasure, it was clarified that the couple would honeymoon with her at her summer residence in South Mountain, Maryland.

Both generations of the Dahlgrens, the Admiral and his wife and John and Elizabeth, lived in New York City. John, a graduate of Georgetown University, practiced civil law. Dahlgren's work was primarily for the City's building department. Realizing the need for standardizing the codes Dahlgren wrote and published Dahlgren's Building Law Manual.

Elizabeth had been raised to high social standards. She knew how to entertain those with money, and where to provide for those without. Under Elizabeth's guidance the young couple soon demonstrated to Mrs. Astor, Queen of New City Society, that they were the next generation of the social 400.

In the second year after they married Elizabeth and John Dahlgren had a son, Joseph Drexel Dahlgren, who died as an infant. In their son's honor the couple donated Dahlgren Chapel to Georgetown University. A year after their first son's death Elizabeth and John would have another son, John Vinton Dahlgren the second.

John Dahlgren died of consumption in August of 1899; he was only thirty-two. Both his parents and Elizabeth's father were already deceased. Elizabeth, who had inherited a share of her father's money, now had gained her husband's share of his family's estate. At thirty-one she was a young, wealthy, widow with one child.

In 1901 Elizabeth was enticed by the dame of society, Mrs. Caroline Astor, to marry Henry Symes Lehr. Lehr claimed to be an actor; his specialty was playing the part of a woman. Born without wealth or linage, Lehr worked for a period as a champagne salesman and bragged of never paying for his own clothes or dinners. He appears to have been Mrs. Astor's pet. His behavior at social events at best would be described as bizarre and at worst distasteful. At one high society event Lehr attended he came with a monkey dressed in a tuxedo. What Elizabeth did not know until her wedding night was that Lehr was gay and had no intentions of consummating the marriage. He did, however, intend to live the highest quality of life on his wife's inheritance.

Realizing her dilemma, Elizabeth wanted to get a divorce and be on with her life. Her deeply devout mother would never permit such a scandal. Elizabeth, who had been raised to believe in family responsibilities and a code of social behaviors, was forced to spend almost thee decades denying her self happiness. To add to the dilemma, Mrs. Astor died and her replacement, Mrs. Vanderbilt, did not find Lehr amusing.

Even with a Drexel at his side Lehr found himself dismissed by America's famous "Four Hundred." The couple spent much of their time in the following years in France where Lehr's lifestyle was more accepted. During World War I, Elizabeth worked for the Red Cross in France and was recognized for her work on behalf of the allied soldiers. Lehr died in 1929 setting the stage for her final marriage.

In 1935, Elizabeth wrote *"King Lehr" and the Gilded Age*. The book was Elizabeth's version of her former husband and the society of which he was enamored but which saw him as a leach. The book was released during the depression and the general public was looking to blame the robber barons. The book became a best seller. Two years later she wrote *Turn of the World*, which was considered the second volume of her tales of society in the Gilded Age.

Seven years after Lehr's death, 67 year old Elizabeth married 68 year old, John Graham Hope de la Poer Beresford 5th Baron of Decies; an Irish peerage. Noted in America as a polo player and yachtsman, Decies had served for twenty years in the British service attaining the rank of colonel. His first wife was the granddaughter of Jay Gould. Although he could have lived out his life serving in the House of Lords, Decies was a man for the people. A friend of the tax payer Decies served as a director of The British Income Tax Payers Association.

The Drexel family was philanthropic especially for educational institutions. They founded Drexel University as a school for students who could not afford a private education. One of Frances' daughters, who had visited this home often in the summer, would enter a convent just before her thirtieth birthday. Her money was tied up in a trust, Sister Catherine helped fund Xavier College (Xavier University); the same woman would fund several Catholic Schools for Native Americans in the southwest. She has been canonized and is Saint Katherine.

Elizabeth's sisters were also socialites. Catherine Drexel married Charles Bingham Penrose; and Lucy married Eric Dahlgren. Elizabeth's youngest sister, Josephine, was the last to marry and was in her own way a woman a hundred years ahead of her time. After Joseph died, his wife realized that she had grown tired of New York. Josephine still loved the city and the culture it provided. She bought her own house and hired a chaperone. She may have been sophisticated but she was not foolish (she knew how an unsupervised single woman would be treated by society). For several years she lived the life of a young woman in the city. Her wedding in the mid 1890s was attended by all those of wealth and power in New York. She was Mrs. William Seton Henry.

The male line of the Drexel's family virtually disappeared.

BROADWAY

717

McConihe

Isaac McConihe was the son of a judge by the same name in Rensselaer County. McConihe graduated from Hamilton College in 1849; returning to his native city of Troy where he engaged in the wool trade. Considered a shrewd businessman, McConihe had soon accumulated a significant fortune.

A Democrat in a city dominated by that party, McConihe felt the call of politics. While only in his twenties, he was twice elected as an alderman for his ward. He gave up the position of alderman to become the police commissioner. In 1860 his career had continued and he was the Mayor of Troy. When Steven Douglas, the Democratic candidate for President, came to the city to give a campaign speech, McConihe introduced him to his constituents.

Twice McConihe showed unusual bravery. In the 1850s there was an unusual race riot in Troy. A group of bounty hunters had captured an escaped slave intending to take the man south for the reward. When the judge ordered that the man be sent south, abolitionists organized to prevent the man being taken from the city. A riot broke out and McConihe was seen among the throng trying to restore order.

During the Civil War the number of men volunteering for service did not meet the northern demand. To increase the number of soldiers a draft was created in 1863. In several northern cities, including Troy, anti draft riots erupted. Although he was no longer mayor, McConihe was again recognized among those rioting as a man calling for order.

Governor Morgan appointed McConihe Mustering Officer for Rensselaer and Washington County.

McConihe and Edward Murphy Jr. (see Hammill Cottage) would constantly compete for control of the Democratic Party in Troy. In the press, McConihe was considered the more reasonable politician with tendencies toward avoiding political dominance and corruption. Their children would ultimately resolve the dispute when McConihe's only daughter married Edward Murphy's son.

In the 1890s, virtually the entire McConihe family would leave Troy and move to New York City where Isaac died suddenly in 1903. The family continued to own the house in Saratoga.

BROADWAY

718

French

This was the home of what would have to be considered the epitome of the American version of the Victorian father and gentleman, Winsor French. Winsor was born in Vermont in 1832. The French family moved to a farm in the Town of Wilton when Winsor was four years of age. Like the children of most farm families, Winsor attended the local public school. With eight brothers and sisters Winsor would have to pay for his own education. He would be 26 before he finished college. When the Civil War broke out he enlisted as a lieutenant but would serve most of the war as the colonel who led the local troops (77th NY). His bravery on the battlefield was so exceptional that, even after he was discharged, he was promoted by an act of congress to general. Returning from the war he resumed his law practice and married. The couple had two daughters and a son. As his luck would have it he had survived some of the bloodiest battles of the war to lose half his family in a matter of a dozen years.

Winsor French was a man with deep roots in America. Even among those in Victorian Era Saratoga who considered themselves America's aristocrats, and in many ways this section of Broadway is a monument to those people, there was probably only one who could claim to be descended from the first "martyr of the American Revolution." Gen. Winsor B. French was that person. His great-great-grandfather, Nathan French, was killed on March 13, 1775 (The attack on Lexington and Concord happened a month later). Nathan and a group of his neighbors were trying to disrupt the British Courts by conducting what today would be considered a sit-in at the local courthouse. The men, who did not want the court to try cases under British laws, were armed with only clubs. The commander of the troops sent to "liberate" the courthouse ordered his men to open fire on the building. Nathan and one other man would die of their wounds in an incident referred to as the Westminster Massacre. Winsor's grandfather, also named Nathan French, served as a lieutenant under George Washington.

On his mother's side, French could trace his roots to Roger Williams, one of the founders of Rhode Island. Winsor, spelled without the "d" was the maiden name of French's maternal grandmother.

French's parents migrated from Rhode Island to Vermont, where Winsor was born. When he was four they moved to a farm in the town of Wilton; the year was 1836. One of nine children, Winsor was the only one to remain in the area. The remainder of his siblings that survived to adulthood moved to the Midwest. Working part-time as a teacher and earning extra money by giving music lessons, French was able to graduate first from Woodstock Academy then in 1859 Tuft's College (age 26). His fraternity brothers in college included historian William L. Stone, and the future Secretary of State John Hay.

Freshly out of college French returned to Saratoga to study law in the office firm of McKean and Pond. French was admitted to the bar in 1861, just two months before the outbreak of the Civil War.

When Lincoln called for troops, French's law mentor, James McKean, set about raising a division which would become the 77th New York; also called the Bemis Heights Regiment. For his efforts McKean would be given the rank of colonel. At the age of 29 French helped raise Company D of the 77th. His efforts earned him the rank of lieutenant upon enlisting and captain upon being mustered into service. During the war McKean's health would fail resulting in his discharge. Winsor was promoted to the rank of colonel to replace his mentor; later he would be a brevet general. He went by both titles, occasionally Colonel but most often was referred to as General French.

French's service during the war was always impressive. There are four battles on which a significant record exists. The Battle of Fort Stevens in July 1864 took place in the District of Columbia. This engagement was the closest southern troops ever came to the nation's Capital. French and his company were rushed back from the siege of Petersburg, Virginia to help defend the Capital. During the battle that ensued, the 77th New York and French were considered instrumental in forcing Confederate General Jubal Early to retreat. It is worthy of note that Lincoln, who came to the fort to watch the battle, was recognized by the southern troops who then began shooting at the President – this is the only case where an American President came under enemy fire while President.

French also served with distinction at the Battle of Cedar Creek. It was in this battle that the Union Army had been trying to charge, at close ranks, across and an open field in an effort to take an old stone factory. After two previous attacks by other troops had been beaten back, General Getty ordered Col. French and his fresh troops to lead a charge. French responded "I cannot take my brigade over that field slowly." To which Getty responded, "Then go quickly." French's men heard him calling over and over "Come on boys," as they charged at a run across the field. During the entire advance French was noted for being at the front of his men. The 77th New York successfully routed the Confederates and had them running toward a creek. The exhausted 77th were relieved when Custer's Calvary took over the chase.

French's behavior was similar at a battle called Mayrs Height. During that charge and despite heavy enemy fire, French was seen riding on his horse back and forth in front of his men encouraging them forward. When he and his men finally captured the Confederate battery, French stood on one of the cannons congratulating his men. General Howe came riding up calling out "Noble Seventy-seventh, to-day you have covered yourself with glory."

It was at the battle of Fort Royal that French's heroism was most noted. Union General Bidwell was killed early in the battle. As senior officer French assumed command of the Union forces until General Sherman could arrive. French's men described him later as "equal to the emergency." This was the same battle where Luther Wheeler was killed (630 Bd.).

During the war French was wounded twice, yet never left the field – a distinction that was always noted as a mark of bravery. On one occasion the combination of stress and unhealthy conditions resulted in French being sick for over a month. To recuperate French was sent back to Saratoga; he spent the time trying to get fresh recruits to replace the men that had been lost.

Probably eligible of a medical discharge, French served his entire enlistment. French's officers so admired his bravery that during the war they gave him a sword inscribed, "He fights for his country." The monument in Congress Park that is a memorial to the Seventy-seventh was half paid for by the men in the company, the remainder paid for by French. The soldier on the monument bears a strong resemblance to French.

After his enlistment expired, French returned to Saratoga where he became a partner in his old firm which was renamed McKean, Pond and French. Like many ex-servicemen following that war, Gen. French used his military service to help him enter politics. In 1868 he was elected District Attorney. More of a civil than criminal lawyer French refused to run for re-election. In addition to being an attorney he would eventually become vice president of the United States Mutual Accident Association, the largest accident insurance company in the world at the time.

It was while French was District Attorney that he once more showed the courage that he had demonstrated frequently as an officer during the war. French called Assemblyman Ray to testify on an issue unrelated to his service for the legislature. Ray refused claiming privilege as a legislator. French boldly had him arrested for failure to appear – it was the first case in the state where there was such a conflict of branches of the government. Called before the legislature to defend his actions, French and the judge who signed the warrant defended their behaviors with the outcome called the Breach of Privilege case. Ray was required to testify.

After actively supporting the election of President McKinley, French was appointed Postmaster in 1899 and served in that capacity until 1903.

French married Emma Pitcher of Cavendish, Vermont on June 2, 1868. He had met her through a branch of his family who lived near Cavendish. The couple had three children; Georgiana (1870), Emma (1873) and Winsor Pitcher (1875). French's wife, Emma, died on News Year's Eve, 1875, three months after the birth of her only son. For the next eleven years French lived in this house as a single father. In 1885, the French family was struck by death a second time when the twelve year old daughter Emma died.

Fifteen months after the loss of his daughter, Winsor married Frances Morris Shepard, the daughter of his neighbor, a Troy banker. Frances was a graduate of Troy Female Seminary (Emma Willard). She would bring wealth and a second son to the house. It appears Frances was a good stepmother to French's two remaining children. For years Frances and her step-daughter, Georgiana, would host grand parties in the house and on the lawn.

A year and a half after Winsor and Frances married she gave birth to William A. Shepard French. Twelve years younger than his brother, Shepard, the name he would use, was almost an only child.

The French family was serious but not all business. Throughout his life Winsor was always active in veterans' affairs including being a charter member of the American Legion post, participating in social activities in the community, was a member of the Saratoga Musical Association and was one of the first members of the Saratoga Golf Club.

Georgiana was an independent woman for the times. Tall, blonde and described as both attractive and graceful, she traveled extensively following her father's second marriage. Shortly before leaving for Glasgow in 1894, Georgiana had an interesting experience that led to the arrest of a serial thief. She had gone to New York City to visit a friend she had made one summer in Saratoga. One day as she entered her bedroom she found what she believed to be her $500 diamond ring laying on the floor. The stone was missing from the setting and broken glass had been left on the floor as if to imply that the diamond had been somehow smashed. The *Times* referred to the act as one of "ignorance combined with cunning." When the detective was called he found that one of the maids had been in the room while Georgiana was out. After the maid's arrest she admitted the deception and said the missing diamond was in the toe of an old shoe. Searching the maid's room they found both the diamond and two other old pawn tickets both for pieces of jewelry.

In 1896, Georgiana became Mrs. John Andrew Harris in a wedding that was one of the social events of the season in Saratoga. Her father, the former music teacher, engaged a male choir of fifty members to sing from the time she stepped out of the carriage until she walked into the church.

The Harris family was from Chestnut Hills, a wealthy section of Philadelphia. J. Andrew, as he was called, was at the time the treasurer of the Lehigh Valley Railroad. John, who was named for his father, would later become a broker specializing in bonds. The senior Harris was the rector of St. Paul's Church in Chestnut Hills. Despite having a congregation among the wealthiest in the area, the elder Harris was vice president of the Civil Service Reform League and a leader in social causes.

Georgiana would have two children; a son and daughter. At least through the 1920's, she never had less than three servants.

It looked for a while like French's son, Winsor (different middle name so not a junior), was going to be even more successful than his father. Raised in the shadow of his father Winsor learned the responsibility to do one's duty. When the Spanish American War broke out he volunteered to serve. Like his father he was commissioned as a lieutenant. While going through advanced training in the south, Winsor developed malaria. He was discharged without actually going to Cuba.

Returning home Winsor joined his father in the practice of law. If his sister had married well, Winsor married very well. His wife was the daughter of George B. Ide, one of the most successful shirt manufacturers from Troy. The Ide family always rented a summer cottage in Saratoga. The younger Winsor French and his wife had three children and built one of the first houses on Marion Place – the house is now gone.

In late 1907, Winsor experienced a particularly bad reoccurrence of the malaria. To recuperate he took a trip south in search of warmer climates. Within days of his return in January of 1908, he became much worse. Winsor died before reaching his thirty-third birthday from meningitis.

The elder Winsor French, who was 75 when his son died, never recovered from the emotional stress. In March of 1910, the senior Winsor French died suddenly. It was exactly two years, two months and two days after his son; apparently the loss was too much.

Shortly after his death French's second wife, Frances, and their son, Shepard, moved to California.

BROADWAY

719

Fuller

Joseph Fuller was the senior partner in the firm of Fuller & Warren a stove manufacturing company in Troy. The stoves they produced were sold under the name Clinton Stoves.

A noble man, Fuller lived the last ten years of his life with business issues and in the midst of controversy, some of which he brought on himself and some of which was a result of the times in which he lived. The labor problems that he experienced were a result of his times, while one of his gifts would create problems because of its perceived conflict of interest. Either of the two stories could be at least an article or in the case of the donation it could possibly be a book. Naturally there had to be political difficulties to add to his frustrations.

His business problems were the result of two fires, one in 1879 the other in 1883. Both blazes caused considerable damage and neither was fully insured. Although fires were relatively common in the wood framed buildings, Fuller never kept his insurance at current value causing him serious losses.

In the late 1880s the Knights of Labor were trying to ensure that they were supported. The union set about trying to control companies not only by striking but by setting up boycotts of the products of unsupportive companies. The union maintained that Fuller & Warren engaged in two practices that were in violation of its positions. The company had a contract to use prison labor to manufacture some of its stoves (a common practice of the times). The union also maintained that the Fuller & Warren were blacklisting some union members.

The Knights solution was to engage in a boycott of Fuller & Warren products. Not only did the union want to have its members avoid purchasing the stoves, union representative went to distributors and told them that if they did not stop selling Clinton Stoves, they would close the stores. When one store in Philadelphia resisted the union took the next step. The union went to all the newspapers and called on their employees to go on strike unless their newspaper stopped carrying advertisements for the store in question. A rift within the union occurred when the newspaper employees failed to go along claiming that since Fuller & Warren and the store in question both employed union members the newspaper workers would not support the boycott.

There was a lot on the line. Fuller & Warren were believed to employ over 12,000 people in its factories in Troy, Chicago, San Francisco, and Cleveland. A standoff developed and after 18 months Fuller & Warren signed a letter of agreement that it would not stand in the way of the union. The union agreed to stop all attempts at a boycott.

It is sometimes what is left out that is as significant as what is included; this is the case in Fuller's obituary. The newspapers listed that Fuller was on the board of trustees of the United National Bank of Troy; a trustee at Troy Female Academy (Emma Willard); and on the board of the orphanage in Troy. What was missing was that he had previously been a member of the Board of Trustees for Union College.

The problems developed when the faculty of the college started having issues with the president, Dr. Potter. The faculty pushed to have the college's president removed from office. The issues were numerous and divisive. Potter had proven to be an excellent fundraiser. So successful were his efforts that less than a fourth of the students were required to pay the full tuition. There were of course issues regarding how the newly acquired money had been used.

As a gesture of support for Union College, Trustee Fuller donated a house reported to be worth $10,000. The house was to be used as the residence of the President. The cost of the house would have made it one of the most valuable properties in Schenectady at the time. Fuller's gift caused considerable dissension among the trustees. As with any board, there were altruistic members who argued that the money could have been spent in more useful ways. There were other more business oriented members who felt that there should not be an issue since the college was economically sound. The real problem was the secondary reason for the gift. Dr. Potter was married to Fuller's daughter. In effect Fuller was providing his daughter with a more suitable home. It took two years and political maneuvering for the faculty to prevail but eventually Potter did leave the college.

In 1880, a group of businessmen organized in an effort to improve Troy's image; Fuller was one of the leaders. It was their contention that the then mayor, Edward Murphy (Hammill Cottage), was using his office to appoint people who were owed political favors. So serious was the problem that in a letter sent to the newspapers, those who were going to supervise the election included the; "very worst class and include gamblers, thieves, ex-convicts, and men who are at liberty only by the suffrage of corrupt police." The claim went on to point out that at least a couple of the pole watchers were not even able to "read and write."

The businessmen of Troy tried to take back what they saw as disruptive behavior by the politicians; chief among them Murphy. On Election Day, Murphy was reelected but it was the subplots that added to the excitement. The Troy police arrested several United States officers releasing them after the ballots had been collected (the inference being that some results were destroyed). When the federal officers were released they promptly filed charges against the city officers bringing them before the federal courts.

Fuller and his wife had three daughters one of whom stood for the cause of women. Daughter Mary, who never married, is most noted for starting Wiawaka, a resort for women working in the textile mills. In 1903 with the help of George Peabody, of Cluett and Peabody (the shirt manufacturers), and Spencer Trask and his wife Katrina, Mary established Wiawaka, which means the "great spirit of women." With the cost of a person's stay based on her income, for the first time working women had the opportunity to enjoy a vacation.

Wiawaka is still in operation today.

BROADWAY

720

Ellis

William Ellis and his family were among the few people from Schenectady to have a cottage in Saratoga.

The Ellis fortune was based on the manufacturing of steam engines. Their primary markets were railroad locomotives with additional business producing steam engines for ships, riverboats, and even engines to power factories. In the early 1850s, John Ellis, William's father, in conjunction with other Schenectady businessmen, raised $50,000 to open the Schenectady Locomotive Works. In 1851 the Schenectady Company commenced the manufacturing of a series of railroad engines; producing five that first year. Initially the company was only marginally successful.

Several years later John Ellis, who was somewhat obstinate, and his partners became embroiled in a fight over control of the company. In a bold move he bought out most of the other stockholders resulting in the Ellis family holding the majority of the stock. Daniel McQueen (30 Union), vice-president of the company, also owned stock. In 1861, under John Ellis' leadership, the company manufactured a total of thirteen locomotives; a 250% increase.

During the Civil War troops and supplies needed to be moved quickly. The need for rapid deployment resulted in lucrative times for those in the railroad business. For the four years of the war, the federal government bought all the engines the Schenectady Locomotive Company could produce: 40 a year (triple their previous production). Forty years later the company's annual production was over 1,000 engines, 400 for locomotives, the rest for other uses. The company also employed over 3,400 people.

One of the key employees and a major stockholder was Daniel McQueen (30 Union). McQueen, like the stockholders years before, had a falling out with Ellis. McQueen left Schenectady Locomotive and started his own locomotive company literally down the street. The two families worked out their differences and McQueen rejoined the Schenectady Locomotive Works. One of John Ellis' sons, Edward, represented the company's interest in New York City. Fearing that someone else might want to start a railroad factory at the site McQueen had been using, Edward approached a bright inventor and developed an offer for him to set up a factory in Schenectady. The inventor was Thomas Edison and his company would become General Electric.

John Ellis, the founder of the company, died in 1864 and over the course of the next 45 years his four sons would each assume the presidency of the company. William, the owner of the Saratoga house, was the treasurer of the locomotive company for many years and the last member of the family to serve as the company's president, 1897 to 1901. William supervised the family's interest in a merger with six other railroad manufacturers into the American Locomotive works headquartered in Schenectady. After the merger, the Ellis family was effectively out of the management of the combined business. The company continues today as Alco Company.

The Ellis family's connection with Saratoga went beyond the house built by William, extending into the next generation. The four Ellis brothers had only two sons between them. The cousins, Bud and Edward, were best friends. There is a line associated with inherited money. The first generation makes it; the second generation keeps it; the third generation spends it. This succession applies to the Ellis men. John Ellis made the fortune; his four sons maintained it; and his two grandsons did their best to enjoy the fruits of the labors of their ancestors.

The cousins' problems were their associates and where they chose to socialize. Both these choices were an embarrassment to the family. The older of the cousins, J. Elmer "Bud", was well known in the Tenderloin district of New York City. During the Gilded Age it is claimed he spent a fortune on the pleasures of this region. His cronies were, like himself, the sons of industrialists. His friends were afloat in a world where they could not keep pace with the memories and images of their fathers in the business world, but wanted to make their own mark at something. Their marks were as big spenders. So serious were Bud's behaviors that when his father died, the estate was left in trust for Bud, not allowing him access to the principle. Bud proved his father's perceptions correct wildly marrying the actress Eva Long after spending his allowance on other pleasures. Although everyone knew Bud suffered from typhoid fever, when he died in 1901, reporters were unable to determine the location. The impression was clear; wherever he died was someplace that would further embarrass the family.

After Bud died, Edward Jr., the remaining male cousin, decided it was time to restore his health and life in general. Even though he was in his late twenties, when his cousin died, Edward enrolled in Yale. During the summer he came to boxing camp near Saratoga Lake to build up his body. The camp was run by the middle weight boxer "Kid McCoy." McCoy introduced Edward Ellis to Estelle Earle. In less than two months Estelle would become Mrs. Edward Ellis.

Six months after the wedding Edward contracted a cold that within days became pneumonia. He died three days after the diagnosis. His widow was suddenly worth between three and six million dollars. She waited just six months to become Kid McCoy's fourth wife. They would later divorce and McCoy would be married a total of eleven times to nine different women; he married one several times.

The four sons in the middle generation of the Ellis family were philanthropic; one of their principal recipients was Ellis Hospital in Schenectady.

BROADWAY

722

Kilmer

This was the house used as the set for the 1961 movie "Ghost Story" staring Fred Astair and Douglas Fairbanks Jr. This is also the only house in the city that has two towers.

For almost sixty years, the man who lived in this house performed immeasurable services to the community, yet was not from the city. Over his lifetime Clarence Kilmer served as justice of the peace, chairman of the City's Planning Commission; a director of the Chamber of Commerce and assistant district attorney.

Kilmer was born in Rock City Falls where his father was the sole proprietor of the Big Falls Mills. His father also owned over a thousand acres of forest near Lake Desolation so Kilmer could not claim a humble birthright.

Acquiring the best public education was not possible in Rock City Falls so Kilmer was sent to live winters with his grandfather in New York City. After graduation from a New York City high school Kilmer attended the City College followed by New York Law School.

An excellent athlete Kilmer was the catcher on his college baseball team; ran track and played on the North American champion lacrosse team. Later in his life he would become an avid golfer and be an officer in the Saratoga Golf Club and President of McGregor Links. He enjoyed golf so much each year he would go to Pinehurst. Kilmer was also a member of the Elks Club where he was an Exalted Ruler.

After graduation from law school, Kilmer moved to Saratoga becoming a partner with Walter P. Butler. The firm's name and partners would change several times while Kilmer was a member.

A trial lawyer, Kilmer was elected president of the Saratoga County Bar Association 19 times. He also took part in the State Bar Association including being involved on committees looking at the bar exam and the selection of judges.

Kilmer served as the deputy fuel administrator for the fourth district of New York State; one of Kilmer's decisions while serving in this capacity would make the *New York Times*. There was a coal shortage in the winter of 1922-23. Learning that coal was passing through the county bound for Canada, the train was stopped. After extensive discussion the railroad was allowed to leave provided they left a car load of coal behind. The next day the coal was unloaded and taken to citizens in the county. The uproar continued until the federal government arranged for almost 300 car loads to be sent to the region the next day.

Kilmer was a fan of horse racing and for a period was the counsel for the Saratoga Racing Association. It was said that for many years he was at the track every morning it was open to watch the horses exercise then later in the day to watch the races.

Kilmer married Frances Mason from North Granville. They had two sons Clarence Jr. and Donald.

BROADWAY

740

Hathorn

Built about 1880, for ninety years this was the home of three generations of the Hathorn family. In addition to having a spring bear their name, for almost a century the Hathorns had the distinction of being one of the families that comprised the entrepreneurial backbone of Saratoga. They also show the difference between being from the village and being for the village.

Henry Hathorn, patriarch and first generation, was born on a farm in the town of Greenfield. Henry had this house built after a long and successful career in a variety of commercial businesses.

Henry moved into Saratoga in the 1830s where he opened a tailor shop, eventually expanding into a dry goods store. Seeing better opportunities in the hotel business, in 1849 Henry sold his store to become part-owner of what was the Union Hotel, later to be known as the Grand Union Hotel. After five years at the Union (1854), Hathorn sold his interest to purchase part-ownership of the Congress Hotel.

The night before it was to open in 1866, the Congress Hotel burned to the ground. The United States Hotel had burned the previous year; reconstruction had not begun due to complex estate issues. Realizing the negative impact of a resort with two of its largest hotels in rubble and being **for** the village, Henry Hathorn immediately began to rebuild. While excavations for a new foundation were underway a spring was discovered that was noted for its high mineral content. Hathorn had the spring tubed and its waters can still be tasted today at the pavilion on Spring Street across from Congress Park.

Henry Hathorn was also a politician serving as county

sheriff from 1853-1856 and returned to the office during the Civil War when the county was lacking in man power (1862-65). In between his stints as sheriff, Hathorn served four terms as a county supervisor. For two terms, beginning in 1872, he was a Congressman. His health failing, Henry did not stand for re-election in 1876 returning to Saratoga instead to build this house and attend to his business interest. After Henry died in February of 1887, his widow, Emily, their son, William, and his wife, Caroline moved to 124 Phila Street. This house became the residence of the Hathorn's other son, Frank.

Frank Hathorn was born in 1847. He was a graduate of Yale. At 37 Frank married 35 year-old Kate Fonda of Kentucky. They waited five years to have their one daughter, Florence. When his father passed Frank took over the management of the family's spring and the operations of the hotel. Eventually the family sold the hotel. His brother's role seems to have been more with the operation of the spring.

Although he was active in support of philanthropic interests, Frank's political career was brief serving only as village supervisor.

In 1912, during one of Saratoga's darker economic periods, Frank Hathorn was concerned about the impact of some of the hotels not opening for the season. Being **from** the village, he unwisely risked a considerable portion of the family money repurchasing the Congress Hotel for $100,000. The stress of the undertaking was too much for Frank who died in the spring of 1913. Following Frank's death the Hathorns sold the Congress Hotel to the city.

How far had Saratoga property values dropped? Forty years before (1873) the Grand Union had been purchased by Alexander Stewart for $560,000. Stewart immediately invested an additional $100,000 in improvements; it was now worth under $300,000.

Florence, who was unmarried when her father died, took over the family's business interests. In January of 1918 America was involved in World War I. Florence and a woman friend named Mrs. Stuart Don purchased a Ford ambulance and presented it to the Red Cross. There was a hitch to their gift; they came with it. The two women had volunteered to be military ambulance drivers in France. One of the requirements of a driver was the ability to take apart and reassemble the engine. The women borrowed a car from the local Ford dealership and spent two days in the Hathorn's garage disassembling and reassembling the auto.

Later in 1918, at the age of 28, Frances married Reginald Durant the publisher of the *Saratoga Sun*. Durant only lived for a few years after the marriage. Following Durant's death, Florence married a businessman from New York City named Sidney Smith. The Smiths lived in New York and maintained this house as a summer cottage until Sidney retired. In retirement they returned to Saratoga year-round. Florence outlived Sidney and she stayed in the house until the 1970s.

BROADWAY

743

Griffith

In the Victorian Era women, especially those who were born to great fortunes but did not marry, often spent their adult life not only partaking of the arts but also working with charities and being responsible philanthropists. In many ways this was exactly the lifestyle of Susan Dannet Griffith who had this house built in either 1916 (her obituary) or 1920.

The Griffith Family's money was based on the brewing of beer in New York City. The family's fortune was from her uncle Daniel Jones who was the largest brewer in the City. In 1881, Daniel died without having any children of his own. He left his four sisters and his brother, John, equal shares in his ten million dollar estate. One of Daniel's sisters was Mary Griffith, the mother of Susan.

There were three children in the family of Griffith William Griffith family (the father's first and last name were the same). The brother's name was Daniel; the choir at Bethesda Episcopal Church is named in his honor. The two sisters were Susan and Margarette. Raised in Manhattan, both Susan and Margarette were educated in private schools where they were given an appreciation for music and the arts. Neither sister ever married.

Their mother's surviving brother, John, died in 1905 also without children and left Susan, Margarette and Daniel each one eleventh of his estate. There is no record of how well the fortune survived the combined ravishes of prohibition and the great depression. But we do know that it was in the hundreds of thousands if not millions.

Susan and Margarette lived together their entire lives. The sisters' main home was at 21 West 56th Street New York City. They were often seen at social events and attending concerts and the opera, although their names are not always shown at the same social functions. Like all of those of their social class the sisters traveled each summer, sometimes in Europe and other seasons in the mountains of New England and New York. The sisters first came to Saratoga in the summer of 1909. The year they arrived was also the peak of the actions to close the carbonic gas companies in an effort to save the springs. The coincidence of the year she arrived and the issue with the springs is especially significant in the case of Susan, since she would hold until her death in 1938 that the health and prosperity of the village depended on the survival of the springs.

The first house in Saratoga that Susan and Margarette lived in was 134 Union, which at the time would have been in the immediate vicinity of Skidmore College's old downtown setting. This location may have been the link between the sisters and the college. However the sisters first became interested Skidmore, their commitment was a key element to the welfare of the college. After Margarette died April 17, 1925, she left part of her money, which was claimed to be several hundreds of thousands of dollars, to charities and the annual interest or the remainder of the money to her sister. Susan decided to sponsor a new science hall for Skidmore College in her sister's name. The Margarette Griffith building, which still stands at the corner of Union and Circular, was built to provide labs for the science program.

Susan donated to a variety of charities. She was a large donor to Skidmore College contributing $100,000 during the depression. At the time of her death her gifts to the college were classified as second only to Lucy Scribner. The Griffith family, especially her brother, was also a major provider to Bethesda Church. Susan was also a major contributor to the Working Girls' Vacation Fund of which she was the third vice president. This fund provided an opportunity for shop girls with tuberculosis to stay in the Adirondacks for a month in the summer. Susan was also active in New York City's School Arts League which awarded thirty scholarships a year to students to study commercial art.

Appointed in 1934 to the board of directors of Skidmorefsda College, Susan Dannet Griffith took the role so seriously that in her obituary they were careful to note that she attended meetings until the time of her death.

In 1936 Susan fell at one of the new baths in the park and broke her hip. Her recovery was far better than anyone expected and by the summer of 1938 her time was spent having the chauffer take her on rides in the country.

The fall did affect her lifestyle. Perhaps concerned about being without sufficient help she never reopened the house, choosing instead to spend the next two seasons at what was, at the time, the new Gideon Putnam Hotel.

It was unexpected when on September 28th, 1938 Susan had a fatal heart attack at the Gideon Putnam.

In the 1970s when the great stallion won the triple-crown this was the summer residence of his owner.

In some of the old records the house that stood on this site prior to the Griffith house was referred to as Cornwall Manor.

BROADWAY

754

Lester

Originally built for Judge Charles Smith Lester, this house was later the home of his son, Judge Charles Cooke Lester. To keep the two men separate, their middle initials are consistently used.

Charles S. was born in Massachusetts; his father had moved there following his financial losses as merchant in Montreal. Charles S. was 21 in 1843 when he moved to Saratoga intent on finishing his reading for the law. His political career began in 1859 when he was elected district attorney. He would later be a member of the board of supervisors, president of the village and a member of the board of education. Charles S. served as a county court judge from 1871 – 77. In 1875 he was nominated for the State Supreme Court losing the election by a single vote. At seventy-five, Charles S. was the oldest practicing attorney in the village.

In 1860 Charles S. Lester supported Steven Douglas for President. Lester was selected to bring the candidate from the train station to the Palazzo of the original United States Hotel. Lester performed the task in style using his carriage with four horses. Following Lincoln's election Lester became a Republican.

Without a doubt the elder Lester's most lucrative position was when he became the local agent for Alexander Stewart when he purchased the Union Hotel in 1872. Stewart was one of the wealthiest men in the United States. Through Lester's efforts in Saratoga, Stewart purchased virtually all the land on the block and expanded the hotel. When he was finished it was the Grand Union Hotel and it was claimed to be the largest summer hotel in the world.

The senior Charles had three sons and one daughter. His sons were Charles C., J. Willard, and James. Like their father, all three sons would become attorneys. In addition to a limited legal practice, Willard started a real estate business with his younger brother James. In the late 1880s and throughout the 1890s, the Lester Brothers was the premier company that rented "cottages" for the season. In addition to his real estate business, James was an officer in the National Guard, attaining the rank of general. The only daughter, Susan, married a professor of Greek language and literature at Yale.

Charles C. Lester was active in local politics. He was selected as the delegate to the State Constitutional Convention (1894) and served on circuit court 1902 – 06. Committed to improving education, Charles C. was on the board of trustees for Albany Law School and Union College.

April 18, 1918 was one of the more extreme nights in the lives of the Lester family. The United States had entered World War I and it was early enough in the war that there were positive feelings about the outcome. As General in the National Guard, John Lester was the grand marshal of a Liberty Loan Parade. Every business in the city (it was a city) had shut down so that the employees could take part in the parade. It was estimated that more than six thousand people turned out to either watch or take part. The people of the city were pulled together by a common objective – the defeat of the German Army.

As the parade was drawing to conclusion, word was given to General Lester that he should hurry to his brother's bedside. Judge Charles C. Lester had suffered a heart attack several weeks before and his prognosis had not been good. The General reached his family's house just before his older brother passed into a coma. Hours later, Charles Lester had another heart attacked and died.

In that one evening the family had experienced the extreme high of having a member serve as grand marshal of one of the biggest parades of the decade to losing its oldest member.

BROADWAY

760

Hall

Everyone has is or her own idea of what would constitute a suitable house for retirement. This house was built about 1907 by William Lord Hall and his wife, Lucia, as their northern residence during their leisure years. Hall and his wife had been spending their summers in one of the cottages on Clement (4). Enjoying the village, they decided to build a house that reflected them and their worth. They would have a winter home in Palm Beach.

Born in Connecticut, Hall moved to Troy when it was one of the industrial and financial centers of the country. Like several others who built on Broadway, Hall was a manufacturer and a self made man. Hall was associated with Miller, Hall and Hartwell Company, which employed over 1,000 workers in its operations in Troy, Hoosick Falls, and Fairhaven, Vermont. Like several other manufacturers in Troy, Hall's concern made collars and cuffs for shirts.

In the days before appliances it would take three live-in servants and additional help for the grounds to maintain the Hall Manor. Hall was able to enjoy the home for eleven years, dying in 1918. His wife Lucia lived until 1925. The couple had no children of their own and left the house and their considerable fortune to a nephew (some of us are luckier than others).

This house would serve as the home of the President of Skidmore College for over two decades.

BROADWAY

767

Leake

It only took the year 1848 for the Marvin brothers (3 & 4 FS) to realize that they were not prepared to handle the day to day operations of the bank they opened in the village. The Marvins were smart businessmen and sought out a professional, John Leake, to be the cashier of their commercial bank. Leake, who was living in Albany, came from a family of bankers; his brother was the cashier of a bank in Troy.

In 1849 Leake came to work in the bank that had been organized under the state banking laws; a decade later it would become The First National Bank, reorganized under the federal laws. For the first thirty years under Leake's leadership, the bank paid an average dividend of 7% a year; a considerable return.

By the mid-1870s Leake would be on the board of the bank he helped build for the Marvins. He would also be president of the board of the newly created Union Savings Bank. His service on the boards of two different banks was not an issue at the time because there were two sets of laws, one governing savings banks and a second for commercial banks. John Leake was the president of the village during the Civil War.

The Leakes had a son, Frederick, and a daughter, Jennie. Frederick was too young to participate in the Civil War but did serve in the 22nd New York Volunteer Cavalry after the war. His interest in horses probably explains the fine carriage house and stable in back of the house. John died in 1892; his wife, Agnes, had died eleven years before. Jennie was one of the genteel women never working and living with her parents. Jennie would stay in the house until her death in 1922.

BROADWAY

779

Gage

Through his own professional skills and his marriage to a local heiress, William B. Gage would become a major land holder in the village. Born in Schenectady, William Gage's father, also named William was a master mechanic at the railroad yards in Saratoga. In the early 1850s the senior Gage, who was a volunteer fireman, was so popular that when he left the village for a position in Kentucky the men threw him a reception giving his a silver pitcher and twin goblets. Within the decade the father had moved back to Saratoga where he again associated himself with the railroad companies based in the village. The father would do well enough that he was consistently able to employ a servant to help his wife manage the family.

The builder of this Baroque style house, William B. Gage, started out as a clerk in the United States Hotel. In the middle of the Civil War he took a position for three years as cashier in a hotel in New York City. Returning to Saratoga briefly, he was the cashier at the Congress Hall for one season in the late 1860's. He returned to New York City again as the cashier at one of the leading hotels. By 1870, at the age of 28, Gage was back in Saratoga where he would live for the rest of his life. When he returned to Saratoga he joined in forming the partnership of Thompkins, Gage and Perry. It appears that Gage was primarily responsible for the financial aspects of the operation

The majority share of the United States Hotel was owned by the Marvin Family (3 & 4 FS). Gage would be the proprietor of the hotel for forty-three years; the last three he was the sole manager. A true businessman he was also the president of the local bank that was the forerunner of the Saratoga National Bank; he was also a director of the Adirondack Trust Company. Gage was also wise enough to invest in the G. F. Harvey Company.

Gage married Caroline Marvin the third daughter of James Marvin (3 FS). They had three children two boys; William and James and a daughter Augusta. Like so many of their relatives, the children William and Augusta left Saratoga.

Gage turned gray before he was forty making it difficult to guess his age. His hair color made him appear older than he was while being physically fit making him appear younger. He was known to be a dapper dresser and wearing suits that were made of the finest material and always fashionable. At a time when the proprietors of the hotels actively mixed with the patrons, Gage's gregarious nature and stylish dress was frequently mistaken for availability by the female clientele. He made a point of retaining his reputation by never taking advantage of any offers he may have received.

Gage's daily routine started with drinking two quarts of Hathorn Spring's water – those familiar with the taste of that spring would give him high marks just for this daily feat. He then would sit in the salon of his great house and play the violin for an hour.

At a tax sale in 1876, Gage would purchase the Saratoga Institute, one of the medical asylums in the villag. The cost was $15,000 and he would reopen it as the Lafayette Hotel.

Gage was among the group of prominent business people who, in the 1890s and early 1900s, tried to return to the village some of the glitter that it was already beginning to lose. In conjunction with William Bockes (34 Cr), Henry Hanson, and his business partner Hiram Thompson, he purchased the Congress Spring and bottle making plant (near the geysers). The village also started special events to attract visitors; William entered a horse in the open air horse show of 1895; his wife would have one of the carriages in the 1899 floral show.

His wife fell on News Year's Eve 1913-14, dying as a result of pneumonia a few weeks later. William remained in the house until he died in 1924; his health failed in his final two years.

Like many of his contemporaries he was a Mason and a member of the Knights Templar

BROADWAY

791

Scribner

Born into an affluent family, the woman who built and lived in this house would marry into the family that owned a large publishing house in New York City. Yet a life that one might have expected to be genteel would turn out to be one steeped in deep personal loss. Despite the pain destiny forced upon her, she would ultimately be known for her abundant social generosity.

Born Lucy Skidmore, she was the granddaughter of Jeremiah Skidmore, one of the first coal merchants in New York City. When only a young man her father, Joseph, was made a partner in the family business; one of his brothers would also join the business and it would become Skidmore and Sons. Joseph would remain with the family business for his entire adult life. Her mother was Lucy Anne Hawley, a member of one of the founding families of Connecticut. Her father, Irad Hawley, like so many others with deep roots, had served as a Captain in the War of 1812.

Joseph and Lucy Hawley Skidmore would have two children. Their son, Irad Hawley Skidmore, was named for her father. The boy was born in 1850 and died in 1852. The couple's second child, named Lucy after her mother, was born July 4, 1853. The elder Lucy died on August 2, less than a month after her daughter was born, from complications relating to childbirth.

The mid 1850s was a time of clear distinction between the roles of women and men. In an action customary at the time, with his wife gone Joseph and Lucy moved back into his father's house. Joseph's sister, Mary, was unmarried and Lucy became her responsibility.

Before 1860, Lucy's father, Joseph, had married and was living with his in-laws. His new father-in-law was the Reverend John Krebs, minister at the First Presbyterian Church in Manhattan. Lucy did not move with her father at first, remaining instead with her Aunt Mary in her grandfather's home. This arrangement continued until Lucy was at least seven years old. After Lucy finally did move in with her father, Mary would remain in the family home until her death in 1908 (she never married).

The new step-mother, Anne Krebs Skidmore, was only 15 years older than Lucy. Joseph Skidmore and Anne Krebs would have no children of their own but it is apparent that Lucy and Anne became close. In 1870, Lucy (17), her father (50) and her step-mother (32) were living together in a house attended to by three servants. Although there were women's colleges available, Lucy Skidmore attended a private finishing school.

Charles Scribner, a contemporary of Joseph Skidmore, had started a publishing business in the 1840s. After a series of name changes the publishing house would be called Charles Scribner and Sons. When his health failed in 1870, Charles called his son, John Blair, to come home from Princeton to run the business while he took a trip to Europe in an attempt to recover his health. At first the trip, which included as stay at St. Moritz, was reported to be reviving the publisher's health. Unfortunately, the stress proved too much and Charles (50) died from typhoid in Lucerne, Switzerland in August of 1871. Unexpectedly his twenty-year-old son, Blair, was thrust into the role of head of the family business.

At the time of Charles' death, Scribner and Company was publishing books, many of which were simultaneously being printed in England. The company was also publishing the successful magazine *Scribner's Monthly*. In 1873, under Blair's leadership, the Scribner Company introduced *St. Nicholas*, one of the first periodicals for children. The youth market begun by Blair would become the center of the company's success for three generations.

In 1875, twenty-one year old Lucy Skidmore married twenty-five year old John Blair Scribner. Since his father's death, Blair, as he was called, had managed the family's publishing house but that year he was joined by his younger brother Charles II. Fresh from college, Charles II covered the publishing house while Lucy and Blair honeymooned in Europe.

For the next three years Lucy and Blair lived on fashionable East Forty-Eighth Street. The couple had two children, both of who died as infants.

Just before the holidays in 1878, Blair contracted a case of pneumonia. It was thought that he recovered after a few days, so he returned to his office. In mid-January, the symptoms returned and Blair was confined to his bed. On January 20th his brother and partner, Charles, came to the house for a visit. In response to Charles' concerns for health Blair said, "Cheer up, old fellow; you always look at the dark side; I shall soon be all right again." An arm gesture was followed by a sigh with which Blair died. He was twenty-eight years old. Lucy was in the room at the time of Blair's death.

Unexpectedly, twenty-five year old Lucy Skidmore Scribner was a widow who had lost two children and her mother. Rather than live alone Lucy returned to her father's house.

It would be almost four years before death would strike again. This time it was Lucy's father, Joseph. Around Christmas he discovered that he had an abscess. Within a week he died at age sixty-two. It was New Year's Eve.

Tragedy brings families together or drives them apart. The misfortunes of the past decade helped Lucy and her step-mother, Anne, become close friends and traveling companions. For the next twelve years the two women would live together in New York City and spend their summers at various venues in New England. The two were wealthy and although living a quiet life they always enjoyed the services of several servants.

In early October 1894, fifty-six year old Anne Krebs Skidmore died unexpectedly. Anne's funeral took place in the same place as Joseph's in the family home on Thirty-Eighth Street.

For the next four years Lucy lived a relatively quiet life. She would often travel for her health. In the summer of 1896 she visited Saratoga and in 1897 decided to make the village her permanent residence.

The one scandal in Lucy Scribner's life surfaced in December of 1898 when she was named as co-respondent in the divorce suit filed by the wife of a doctor in California. Able to spend the winters in more pleasant surroundings than those in New England, the court documents claimed that Lucy had spent January through April of 1898 in Pasadena. There she had allegedly engaged Dr. J. C. Fraser as her physician. In a period where she was concerned about her health, Dr. Fraser visited Lucy each day. According to a story in the *Times*, the doctor's wife claimed to have asked her husband to stop visiting Mrs. Scribner but he refused saying she (Lucy) was a "fine woman" and inferred that if he were free he would marry Lucy.

According to the doctor's wife, when Lucy left for the east coast in May of 1898, Dr. Fraser accompanied her first to New York then to White Mountain, New Hampshire where she spent the summer. The initial claim was that Lucy had paid all the doctor's expenses ($4,000) including his tailoring bill. In an effort to show the injustices of the world, the doctor's wife claimed she was forced to live on $30 a month from the doctor and what money she could raise by renting rooms in her Pasadena home.

The very next day after the story appeared there was a very strong defense launched on behalf of Lucy. It seems that the year in question was not 1898 but rather 1891. The difference is more than just seven years: the difference was that in 1891 Lucy was constantly traveling with her step-mother; in 1898 Lucy would have been traveling alone. Lucy admitted that the doctor had been engaged as a physician to accompany her and her step-mother east. She further acknowledged that she had paid the doctor's expenses as anyone would pay for a doctor.

Two years later, under pressure Dr. Fraser's wife withdrew her claim against Lucy, writing a letter of apology which appeared in the *Times*. In the letter the doctor's wife said that she "deplored her misfortune in having been misinformed regarding Mrs. Scribner relationship" with her husband. The wife was granted a divorce based on verbal "cruelty," but Lucy had lived under a tainted veil for two long years. It is not possible to measure the amount of pressure the rumor had exerted on a woman who had tried to live a totally proper life; however, when the period was over Lucy became even more philanthropic.

A new face in Saratoga, Lucy Scribner needed to gather a group of friends. Since she was not employed, her natural link became becoming an active member in her church. There she met other likeminded women who were in a position to support causes. In 1903, the women announced that they had rented buildings across from Congress Park. The group's purpose was to open a free industrial school for girls. The school the women founded would grow to become Skidmore College. Lucy would serve on the board of directors until her death in 1931.

The reason why Lucy chose to call the school by her maiden name, Skidmore, rather than her married name of Scribner was not discovered.

***

Lucy Skidmore Scribner would live in the cottage for thirty years with up to seven servants. It is interesting that in two different census, the servants were all either born or descended from parents who were born in Sweden. In New York City all her servants had been Irish.

***

This house is one of the best examples of a closed circle. Starting out as the home of the founder of Skidmore College it is now the residence of the college's president.

795

Red Stone
Villa

Eli Clinton Clark's life was an economic rollercoaster. While still a relatively young man he inherited his father's lumber business. The operation had two parts; the cutting of raw timber in the Adirondacks and the sales of that lumber in Albany. Within a few years of his inheritance Cark had lost most of the family money. To recover, Clark then went to the Midwest where he made his own fortune again in lumber.

In a position to live in grandeur he and his family returned east living in Ballston Spa until this house was completed in 1886. The house which is considered in the Queen Anne style was designed by S. Clifford Slocum. The original gardens, which were noted in several articles, included the property on which the Scribner house is built (791 Br). The Clark family had their primary residence in New York City where Eli listed his occupation as a banker.

Clark was associated with several local businesses including Clark Mills, near Schuylerville. Toward the end of his life some of his investments lost money. To maintain the house Clark sold off his garden.

Clark, who died in 1913, first married Mary Green of Albany then Mary Scott. He had three sons; Samuel, who moved to Kansas City; Francis, who lived in New York City; and Frederick of Watertown. His two daughters, Mary and Helen traveled throughout Europe before settling in New York City.

The house was then purchased by Frank Nolan, the son of Michael Nolan (30 Cr), who lived in it for over a decade.

BROADWAY

860

Surrey Inn

At the turn of the last century one of the leading investment bankers in the country was E. Clarence Jones. It was the era in banking of J. P. Morgan, the Drexel Brothers and Russell Sage. Jones was a member of the small elite circle of people who could change the value of the stock market just based on where they choose to invest their money. One of the best measures of Jones' wealth is demonstrated by his offer in 1905 to purchase $30,000,000 in Cuban Bonds.

Although Jones preferred to invest in stocks and bonds, he would occasionally take over failing companies. As a banker, Jones was so independent that he was what was referred to as "a one man partner;" each of his partners only held one share of stock; the remainder he held personally. He was sued after forcing two ex-partners to sell their stocks for not allowing them to benefit in transactions they had arranged. Jones won the suit.

One of the more interesting tales about Jones evolves from a widely covered inquiry held in 1906. The focus of the inquiry was Col. W. D. Mann, a Civil War veteran who owned *Town Topics*, a small failing newspaper in New York City. It would be a compliment to call Mann's newspaper a tabloid. Basically, *Town Topics* carried gossip about the city's rich and famous. The reports were rarely complimentary.

Mann who was nearly broke, considered himself "a humanitarian and philanthropist, who had been stripped of his substance through his confiding nature;" few others would be so complimentary. In order to raise funds Mann resorted to two measures both of which were blackmail. In some cases he would borrow from the rich; in exchange for the loan the provider would be considered "immune" from his columns. Naturally he never intended to repay the loans. His other scheme was to ask people to subscribe to *Fads and Fancies*, a publication he was considering creating. Although he was smart enough never to write the details, it was assured that a subscription would mean that the person's name would not appear in the columns. Some of those who either subscribed or lent money were; two of the Belmonts, Vanderbilt, Gould, Flagler, Harry Lehr and of course E. Clarence Jones. Jones lent Mann $10,000 to be assured that an article referring to Jones' wife as a Bowery performer would never appear.

Jones made the news again in 1913 when he was sued by Katherine Cecile Belden for breech of promise. It seems that Miss Belden expected Jones to marry her. Readers will understand the question clearly when they read Miss Belden's mother's name; Kathryn Ballou-Watrous-Fletcher-Brown-Travers; each hyphen represents a marriage. The mother had also lived with a man named Sully by whom she had three children. The family business appears to have been divorce. E. Clarence Jones successfully fought the suit.

When the First World War broke out in 1914, Jones and 400 other Americans were trapped in Baden Baden Germany. Jones and Anthony Drexel made arrangements for passports and letters of credit for their fellow Americans to allow them to leave. Jones also arranged for over 200 British citizens to sneak out posing as Americans.

Jones had divorced his first wife about the turn of the century. For twenty years he was a social king, hosting huge dinners and parties in New York, Palm Beach and Europe. In 1921, he married the widow Margaret Seeley Blossom. She was an actress and appeared in the silent movie "Mr. Jones." This house was built by Jones as a retreat for his new wife and himself.

The house would later be purchased by State Senator Thomas Brown. It was for a brief period a boys' academy called the Brown School. It is currently an administrative building for Skidmore College.

STATE

Hammill
Cottage

Generally, the history of each house is limited to the story of one of its former families. Not so for Hammill Cottage. During the first half century this cottage existed it was the summer home to four families from Troy; each of which warrants recognition. The first two came into their careers and fortunes through their families, while the last two were true Horatio Alger stories. The four families in order were: William Thomas, a manufacture of drugs and chemicals; Edward Murphy, brewer and politician; William Frear, merchant extraordinaire; and Frank Twining, shirt manufacturer.

The first resident, William Thompson, was associated with his family's business manufacturing wholesale drugs, chemicals and medicines. The firm was started by William's father with William and his older brother assuming control. In the late 1800s the firm was one of the three leading drug firms in the State. William was also the trustee on three Troy banks and numerous charitable organizations. He was a director of the Troy Gas Company and Troy & New England Railroad, which he was instrumental in creating.

A politician's politician, Trojan Edward Murphy was the head of several different companies starting with his family's brewery and including such diverse businesses as Troy Gas Company; more importantly he was a United States Senator. Born in Troy, educated in the public schools, Edward Murphy went to St. John's College in NYC. Murphy started his political career as an aldermen in Troy, became Fire Commissioner of the City, then mayor. For two decades he headed the State Democratic Party. He was a U.S. Senator from 1893-99.

There were two periods in the 1800s when there was a review about whether to shift from the gold standard to the silver standard. It was a serious issue with the argument for a solid dollar being heard throughout the country.

Senator Murphy voted to shift to the silver standard. This vote caused him to be censured by the state legislature. When Murphy was a United States Senator they were appointed by their state legislatures. It was not until years later when the constitution was changed to have the election for U.S. Senators directly by the people. While Murphy was Senator, the Republicans took over control of both chambers of the state legislature and Murphy was defeated in his bid for reelection. His vote to shift to the silver standard helped the Republican effort.

William Frear was the model of a merchant extraordinaire. Starting from reasonably humble beginnings in Coxsackie, Frear would rise in status to where he would be considered "Troy's leading merchant." His department store, "Frear's Cash Bazaar" in Troy, was considered the largest store between New York City and Montreal. Based in Troy in a time when travel was either by train or carriage, Frear had customers from as far away as Vermont. Starting with partners, Frear was only 28 when he had bought them out and owned the store by himself. He later would take his brother and two of his sons as partners. Frear Park in Troy is named after the family.

Responsible for all aspects of the business, Frear led his competitors through his knowledge of advertising, mail order business, and the need to diversify and expand the store's product line. Frear was wise and diversified his assets to include a hotel, and extensive real estate holdings. He was on the board of several charities. Active supporter of the Republican Party, Mr. Frear never held political office.

Twining's was a humble to grand story. Starting as a bank clerk, Twining went to work for one of the shirt companies in Troy where, over his lifetime, he rose to president of George Ide Co. Twining was also vice president of a bank, head of the Twining steamer Company, and a major investor in Beacon Electric Company.

STATE

Reverend
Mulford

Without a doubt one of the best examples of siblings taking care of each other is the retirement home of Reverend Joseph Mulford. He was one of the earliest ministers in Christ Church in Troy where he served for over twenty-five years. Although there are examples of ministers who made or inherited enough money to live fairly well, few examples exist of a minister who could live this well in retirement. By comparison to his brothers-in-law he lived humbly.

The source of Mulford's comfortable retirement was his wife's family the Cluetts. Before the Cluetts had anything that approached a fortune, Mulford married Mary Harris Cluett. Mary was the only sister in America with five Cluett brothers. About the time this house was built for the Mulfords, the Cluett men constructed the three Queen Anne's on Clement Street.

Several of Mary's brothers owned Cluett Peabody Company the largest manufactures of shirts, collars and cuffs in the world at the time. The remaining brother owned a piano manufacturing company in Troy that had been started by her father.

Mary was as devoted to social causes as her brothers were to industry. Although much of her work was on behalf of her husband's church, Mary also undertook projects on behalf of the poor. She was said to have had an excellent soprano voice.

Through her family, Mary was in a position to spend her last fifteen winters in Palm Beach and her summers in Saratoga. She died in 1915 in her eightieth year, her husband died in 1920. They had no children.

45

Home of the
Good Shepherd

Nothing would be more inappropriate than to omit the building that was home to more people than any other in the neighborhood. It was a building created to care and comfort elderly women, many of whom had no other safe place to stay. For over one hundred years countless women would consider this great white building their home.

First created in the 1860s, the Home of the Good Shepherd had other temporary locations before a permanent home was erected during the period 1877-99. The idea of a home for the elderly started in the mid-1860s as the result of the efforts of three women; Mrs. Thomas Marvin (4 FS); Mrs. Gibson, wife of the minister at the Bethesda Church; and Mrs. William Bryer White. These women were in the practice of visiting and tending to the poor in Saratoga. Realizing that a need existed for women regardless of faith the three banded together to create the Home of the Good Shepherd. Over the years students from Skidmore College and other organizations have contributed time and energy to the care of the residents of this fine structure.

The Home of the Good Shepherd has moved to more modern facilities near the hospital. This building is scheduled to become condominiums. In 2006 the building was advertised as having 30 bedrooms and one kitchen.

35

Pierson

When Greenfield Avenue was being developed the first houses on the street were all owned by men who had been born in Saratoga; all were lawyers.

William A. Pierson was born in 1859. His family moved to Vermont where he received his education. After graduating from a college preparatory high school, he started teaching near Burlington so that he would be able to attend classes at the University of Vermont. Unable to complete his college courses because of ill health, he returned to Saratoga to read for the law. Admitted to the bar in 1883, Pierson was immediately elected Justice of the Peace. He would later serve on the school board.

Pierson had one client that made a significant difference in his practice. Pierson was the attorney for Seymour Ainsworth, one of the wealthiest men in the village. Ainsworth had been acquiring real estate holdings dating back to when he had been the co-owner of the Union Hotel. Ainsworth built and owned several of the commercial buildings that are still standing on Broadway.

Pierson was not only Ainsworth's civil attorney, but also managed his extensive property. Pierson understood the advantage of renting and every season his cottage was rented.

Pierson was active in the political party. His activity did not include holding office but was more behind the scenes. For several years Pierson was the secretary of the Republican State League.

Pierson and his wife had one son, William Mathews Pierson, a lawyer in Troy.

GREENFIELD

27

Shepherd

This is the residence of Augustine Shepherd, one of three families on Greenfield Avenue where the owners were born, raised and practiced law in Saratoga. The son of Daniel and Mary White Shepherd (42 Cr), Augustine was from one of Saratoga's oldest and wealthiest families. Augustine's mother was the stepdaughter of Dr. John Clark (46 Cr), one of the early owners of Congress Spring.

Augustine's wife, Harriet, was the daughter of Silas Briggs, also an attorney. Harriet was also born and raised in Saratoga. After the family had lived for three generations in the village, the couple's two sons, Augustine Jr. and John, would both move out of the community.

Like his father, Augustine was an attorney having studied under Lemuel Pike (117 Cr). He served as justice of the peace; as the police justice; and for several years was on the board of supervisors. While on the board of supervisors he served on the committee that replaced the county courthouse. He was also the counsel for the village of Saratoga.

Shepherd was a quiet, thin, man. In his early life Augustine was a physically active man serving for seven years in the National Guard and was one of the charter members of the Saratoga Bicycle Club. His health failed him when he was in his fifties forcing him into retirement. He died at the age of 63.

Readers please note: the entire building shown is one house.

22

Diamond Jim
Brady
and
Lillian Russell

Shortly after the United States came into being, our collective heroes were generals and politicians. As individual fortunes began to grow, industrialists and business persons were idolized. Today there are celebrity couples that attract and for some brief period hold the interest of Americans. The public wants to know where these people eat, party, what they wear, and who they associate with. The members of these idolized couples are usually media stars or billionaires. They owe much of this adoration to one couple who visited Saratoga each summer during the Gilded Age. This was the summer cottage of America's first "celebrity couple."

There are people who, because of their antithesis behaviors, are a paradox to describe. Capable of eating more food at each meal than four other men, some would describe him as gluttonous; yet he never consumed alcohol, drank tea or coffee, and of course he never smoked. He was a large man, weighing close to 300 pounds, making him appear obese, yet he was an outstanding dancer. A millionaire bachelor, who spent every evening of the week at the best clubs in Manhattan, qualified him as a dandy; yet, he was at work everyday from 9:00 to 5:00. Born into a humble Irish family he would become so enchanted by fine jewels that one precious gem would become part of his nickname. James "Diamond Jim" Brady was a man of many excesses, yet it is claimed that he never told a lie.

Diamond Jim's paramour had personality, charm and a reputation for enjoying the limelight which matched his. With long naturally blonde hair and a figure once described as "a lot of what men like," she was a star, if not a talent. Born in rural Iowa and raised in Chicago, other than her attendance at a Catholic school, during her lifetime little was known about her youth; and that was just fine with her. An actress in musical comedies, she married four times, yet she never wed the man with whom her name is most commonly associated. She lived a lifestyle that would accurately be described as notorious; yet at her funeral there would be flowers from the President and she would be buried with full military honors. Made famous by her beauty, voluptuous body and her singing voice, she would be one of America's first poster girls; while later she became a champion of women's suffrage. Any honest assessment would hold that Lillian Russell equaled Diamond Jim as a larger than life character.

It appears that Jim really loved her but he loved life even more; her feelings for him are harder to define.

Even with their dynamic personalities, celebrity status, and his immense fortune, the couple was never able to truly break into polite society. The couple attended the theater, ate at the best restaurants, and went to the race track and other public events but they were not invited into the homes of America's 400. The reason may have been their lifestyle. At a time when people tried to at least appear proper, Diamond Jim and Lillian Russell never married, yet were acknowledged as a couple. Seen for years in public together the debate over whether they actually were sexual partners continues even today. It may also have been their love of life that kept them from being accepted in the stodgiest of circles; after all they were regularly written about in the newspapers. While those of wealth tended to want to only have their names in the newspapers in reference to attendance at important events or benefits, Lillian and to some extent Diamond Jim relished their names appearing in the newspaper. The couple's acceptance, although only on the periphery of society, is proof that most people will sanction a different standard given there is sufficient wealth and fame; that is of course, as long as one of the parties is not in politics.

The gifts "Diamond Jim" bestowed on Lillian Russell were reported in the newspapers but were only a minor element to the couple's media glamour. Both were also known for their evenings out and their appetites. Stories of how much he ate are probably true and in general tell of a man capable of eating a week's worth of food at a single meal. The effect of dining with him for years eventually showed in Lillian's dimensions. Starting with a classic hourglass shape, over the years she became more full-figured.

Diamond Jim made his fortune not in owning the railroads but rather in supplying them with whatever equipment they needed. He could furnish the railroad companies with anything from the chairs and tables for the dining car to an entire railroad car. A master salesman, Brady built his success on three key elements: honesty, delivery when promised, and being the kind of person people liked being around. In the vernacular of the day he was a "sporting man." He enjoyed boxing, horse racing, and pool; if you could bet on it, Diamond Jim did.

Brady developed a fondness for jewels, calling his collection his "pets." In all Brady had 21 sets of jewels which he wore in a strict rotation. Brady did not have to repeat a set of jewels for three weeks. Each set was estimated to cost $50,000 and consisted of shirt studs, scarf pin, ring(s), cuff links, belt buckle and cumber bun. One could argue that the most impressive jewel Diamond Jim ever wore on his arm was Lillian Russell.

Lillian Russell was her stage name. She was the daughter of Charles Leonard, the publisher of a small newspaper in Chicago. When she was about 17 Lillian, accompanied by her mother, left the Midwest and moved to New York City. In the city she took voice lessons hoping to perform on Broadway. By the age of 19, she was given a contract as a ballad singer at a salary of $40 a week. Eventually Lillian landed starring roles in "H.M.S. Pinafore" and "The Pirates of Penzance." The title of her musical "The Maid and the Moonshiner" probably best describes her future relationship with Brady.

Lillian married four times. By her first husband, she had a son who died as an infant. By her second husband, she had a daughter, Dorothy, who would play a heavy role in Lillian's later life. Her third marriage was brief. Lillian's fourth marriage was in 1912, after her relationship with Brady had cooled.

Lillian's last husband was a wealthy Pittsburgh publisher named Alexander Moore. It was an interesting marriage from the beginning with Moore spending their honeymoon in Chicago trying to secure the Republican Presidential nomination for Teddy Roosevelt, rather than going off alone with America's sweetheart. When Teddy lost the nomination to the man who had been his own handpicked successor, William Taft, he ran as an independent candidate. Moore became one of Roosevelt's leading press people for the new Bull Moose Party.

By the time of her fourth marriage, Lillian's voice was too exhausted to perform regularly but she was not ready to retire. She had come to enjoy, perhaps even need, to be in front of an audience. After her marriage she continued to do performances to benefit charities but in 1915 her life made a dramatic turn when she made her first speech in favor of women's suffrage. Married and living more sedately in Pittsburgh, Lillian became a writer and spokesperson on women's rights and constantly became more involved in Republican Party politics.

By the spring of 1917, Brady's lifestyle had caught up to him and he was facing serious health issues that had been developing for years. To facilitate his recovery he left New York and took a $1,000 a week apartment on the Boardwalk in Atlantic City. Although a gregarious man, Brady knew the seriousness of his health issues and chose not to see his old friends while he was in Atlantic City. Being one of the country's most notorious businessmen, newspapers regularly reported on his condition. At first it appeared that the sea air was helping him rally but it was too late. The man who supplied Vanderbilt, Harriman and Gould, and who kept company with such beautiful women as Lillian Russell, died in his sleep with only his valet present. At the time of his death at age 61, it was estimated that Brady was worth between ten and twenty million dollars. That would be at least 250 million dollars today. Never marrying or having children, he left his fortune to a variety of charities, primarily hospitals.

The same year Brady died, Lillian was given the rank of colonel in the Marines. The position was an acknowledgement of her efforts to recruit soldiers; sell war bonds; and support the U.S troops in the Great War. After the United States entered World War I, Lillian went to France to raise the soldiers' morale. She was so proud of her military status that beginning in 1917, Lillian Russell often performed in the uniform of a marine colonel.

In the 1920s she was selected by the Secretary of Labor to visit Europe to see if agreements could be worked out under which potential immigrants, with emotional problems, could be screened in their home countries rather than having to be sent back after they reached Ellis Island. During her return trip, Lillian slipped and fell while on board the ship. She died as the result of the injuries that she sustained. Like Brady, Lillian Russell was 61 at the time of her death.

Lillian cast an immense shadow and her daughter had trouble being seen in her own light. Like her mother, Dorothy tried to make it on the stage performing minor roles in musical comedies. Dorothy lacked her mother's dynamic stage persona. Bent on living her own life she married for the first time while still a teenager. By the time she was thirty Dorothy had been married four times (she would later marry at least once more).

In 1915 Dorothy had the dubious distinction of being the first person arrested under New York State's first prescription drug laws – she had forged a doctor's name to obtain morphine. Dorothy had a reason for her depression; she lost a leg as the result of an automobile accident.

Despite of, or because of, her daughter's troubles, Lillian was committed to providing for her security. There is no doubt that there existed a prenuptial agreement in which Lillian's fourth husband, Moore, agreed to provide for Dorothy. In fact, when the rumors that Lillian was engaged to Moore first surfaced; she was quoted as saying that there were details that needed to be worked out first. The record is not totally clear but it appears Lillian thought that Moore would leave half his considerable estate to Dorothy.

Because of the accident on board the ship, Lillian pre-deceased Moore. From the beginning there were problems settling Lillian's estate. First reports listed her worth as in the mid-six digit, but as time went on the value kept decreasing until eventually it was said to be under $40,000. As time passed, it would come out that the reason for the decreases was Moore's claim that most of Lillian's jewels and porcelain were not part of her estate but were in fact his possessions.

Following her mother's untimely death Dorothy went to Europe to recover her health. When she returned Dorothy claimed to have written her mother's biography. After the first couple of chapters appeared in a newspaper, Moore was so angered that he rewrote his will providing only $1,000 for Dorothy. When Moore died, the lawsuits against his estate would continue for years with Dorothy consistently the loser. The issues in question were Lillian's jewelry and porcelain collection. Eventually, Dorothy was financially ruined and went bankrupt.

In 1895, Diamond Jim Brady was the first person in New York City to own an automobile.

Diamond Jim lived with his mother until he was over 40, then had her placed in an asylum.

Diamond Jim's brother bore the dubious nickname of Brass Dan because he was better at losing money than making it.

At Lillian's funeral there was a military volley fired over her casket.

In Saratoga there are several houses that claim Lillian Russell stayed within their walls. They may be correct. The assurance that this was at least one of the houses comes from a letter written by Margaret Hays (581 Br) telling of how as a child she sat on the back porch with Charles Brackett (605 Br) and watched trough the window as Lillian Russell ate breakfast with Diamond Jim.

The house actually belonged to Walter Butler and his wife (596 Br).

ROCK

15

Pond

This house was owned by the Pond/Rich family for at least its first seventy years.

Starting as partner of Judge Charles S. Lester (754 Br), Alembert Pond later created a Law firm with Winsor French (718 Br) and Edgar Brackett (605 Br). The fact that his name consistently comes first among this prestigious group speaks to his skills. Pond was noted for his trial preparations and his ability to present cases before appellate judges. Pond, who was the oldest of the partners, was elected to the state assembly in 1868. The previous year Pond had been a delegate to the state's constitutional convention.

Pond's wife was Elizabeth Curtis Lester; her relationship to Charles Lester (754 Br) has not been established, although their cemetery plots are immediately adjacent to each other. The Ponds had two sons; Byron, who died young and Charles, who attended Union College and became a lawyer. Charles never married and lived in his parents' house until just before his father died. He had recently given up his law practice to become the village street commissioner. When Alembert died in 1896 he left the house to his daughter and her husband. Charles died in 1900.

At the age of 32, Pond's daughter, Sarah, married Waldo Rich. Waldo was the son of Dr. Cyrus Rich who had distinguished himself during his service with the 77th New York. Waldo Rich was a bookkeeper who became a sub-teller at several banks, eventually becoming the teller for the Adirondack Trust Company.

Waldo was a trustee of the Anthenaeum. He died in 1930 and Sarah died in 1933. They had no children and the house passed out of the family's ownership.

Bibliography and suggested Readings

The main sources for this book are the newspapers from the era, the files at the Saratoga Public Library and those at the Saratoga County Historian's office. In most cases the key to learning about a given individual or family was to find the obituary or obituaries and work backward. The newspapers used includes, but is not limited to, *The Daily Saratogian, Saratogian, Troy Times, Troy Press, Albany Evening Journal, Ballston Journal, The New York World* and *New York Times*.

Books

Anderson, George Baker, *Our County and its people: a descriptive and biographical record of Saratoga County, New York*; The Boston History Co. 1899

Anonymous: *Emma Willard and her pupils, or, Fifty years of Troy Female Seminary. 1822-1872*, New York: Mrs. R. Sage, 1898

Anonymous: *History of the Bench and Bar of New York*; New York History Co., 1897

Anonymous: *Hudson-Mohawk Genealogical and Family Memoirs*, New York: Lewis Historical Publishing Company, 1911

Dunn, Violet B., *Saratoga County Heritage*, unknown 1974

Durkee, Cornelius E., *Reminiscences of Saratoga*, unknown 1929

Durkee, Cornelius E.; *Index to Marriage and death notices in the Saratoga Sentinel: 1819-1837*, unknown 1870,

Joki, Robert, *Saratoga Lost; Images of Victorian America*, Black Dome Press Co., Hensonville, New York, 1998.

McGregor, Jean, *Chronicles of Saratoga: a series of articles*, Saratoga Springs, NY: The Saratogian 1947.

Stone, William Leete; *Reminiscences of Saratoga and Ballston*, New York, Worthington Co. 1890.

Sylvester, Nathan Bartlett, *History of Saratoga County, New York:*

with historical notes on its various towns, Chicago, Ill.: Gresham Publishing Co., 1893

Sylvester, Nathan B., *History of Saratoga County New York with Illustrations, and Biographical Sketches, of some of its prominent men and pioneers*; 1878 Philadelphia; Everts and Ensign.

Index of People

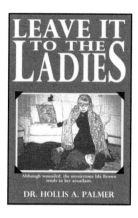

Pictures from the Victorian Era show women in heavy, ornate dresses doing needlework or reading poetry while doting over their perfect children. The reality of these peoples' lives were usually quite different. In this book we learn that there was a group of women bent on revenge, or seeking to be free from the shackles of marital bondage.

In six months she went from being the mistress of a man who was nominated for governor to a person charged in a double homicide. But with her conviction came a curse on the lawyers involved in the trial.

A collection of six stories in which it is known who committed the crimes but they all got away because of the Rules of Victorian society.

An Irish maid whose murder rattled a small village, but not as much as the suicides, five years later of four successful male friends.

A collection of three stories. From a bank robbery to mass murder, these stories are based on the trials that made the lawyers famous enough to be in the Billings's trial.

Although the evidence was weak, the wealthiest man in a very rich county, Jesse Billings, was charged with the murder of his wife. This was one of the first trials covered by the national press.